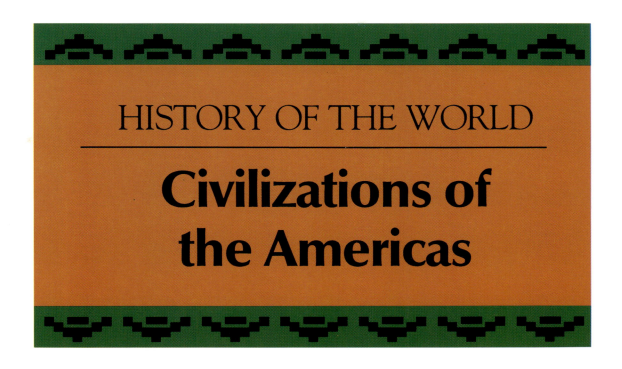

# HISTORY OF THE WORLD

## Civilizations of the Americas

CHERRYTREE BOOKS

A Cherrytree Book

This edition adapted by
A S Publishing

First published by Editoriale Jaca Book s.p.a. Milan
© Editoriale Jaca 1987
First English edition published in United States
by Raintree Publishers
English translation © Raintree Publishers Limited Partnership
Translation by Hess-Inglin Translation Service

This edition first published 1990
by Cherrytree Press Ltd
a subsidiary of
The Chivers Company Ltd
Windsor Bridge Road
Bath, Avon BA2 3AX
Reprinted 1993

Copyright © Cherrytree Press Ltd 1990

British Library Cataloguing in Publication Data
Civilizations of the Americas.
   1. North & South American civilization, to 1599.
   I. Williams, Brian II. Series III. Preistoria e civilta
   delle Americhe, *English* 970.01

   ISBN 0-7451-5106-X

Printed in Hong Kong by Imago Publishing Ltd

All rights reserved. No part of this publication may be reproduced,
stored in a retrieval system, or transmitted, in any form or by any
means without the prior permission in writing of the publisher, nor be
otherwise circulated in any form of binding or cover other than that in
which it is published and without a similar condition including this
condition being imposed on the subsequent publisher

# Contents

| | |
|---|---|
| The Physical Americas | 4 |
| The Discovery and Settlement of America | 5 |

## NORTH AMERICA

| | |
|---|---|
| Early Americans | 6 |
| The Intermountain Area and the West Coast | 8 |
| The Northwest Coast | 10 |
| Ancient People and Early Farmers in the American Southwest | 12 |
| The Anasazi | 14 |
| The Great Plains | 16 |
| Peoples of the Southeast Regions | 18 |
| The Northeast Woodland | 20 |
| The Mississippian People | 22 |
| The Arctic | 24 |
| The People of the Subarctic | 26 |

## MESOAMERICA

| | |
|---|---|
| Early Inhabitants | 28 |
| The Central Plateau of Mexico | 30 |
| Religious Centres of the Central Plateau | 32 |
| The Teotihuacan | 33 |
| The Toltecs | 36 |
| The Aztecs | 37 |
| The Olmecs | 40 |
| The Zapotecs | 42 |
| The Mixtecs | 43 |
| The Maya | 45 |
| A Mayan City: Chichén Itzá | 46 |
| Veracruz | 48 |

## SOUTH AMERICA

| | |
|---|---|
| Early Inhabitants: Paleolithic Hunters and Gatherers | 50 |
| Early Farmers and Potters | 53 |
| The Northern Andes | 54 |
| Andean Civilization | 56 |
| On the Eve of the Incas | 59 |
| The Inca Empire | 60 |
| The Southern Andes | 62 |
| People of the Caribbean, the Amazon Basin, and Eastern and Southern Brazil | 64 |
| The Chaco, the Pampa, and Uruguay | 66 |
| Southern Chile, Patagonia, and Tierra del Fuego | 68 |
| Glossary | 73 |
| Index | 77 |

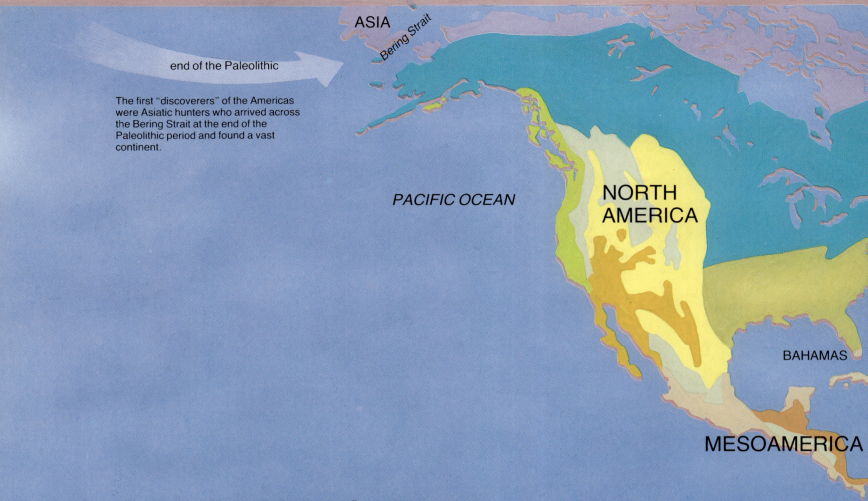

end of the Paleolithic

The first "discoverers" of the Americas were Asiatic hunters who arrived across the Bering Strait at the end of the Paleolithic period and found a vast continent.

grasslands
subtropical plains
deserts
tropical rain forests
tropical savannas
ice
arctic tundra
subarctic regions
high mountains and plateaus
coastal regions with a distinctive climate

# THE PHYSICAL AMERICAS

The New World landmass measures 14,500 kilometres (km) from the Arctic to Cape Horn. The two continents, North and South America, reach 4,800 kilometres across at their widest points. This immense territory covers one-quarter of the world's habitable surface.

The most impressive feature in North America is the Rocky Mountains, which run the length of the continent like a gigantic backbone. The Appalachians, a more ancient mountain chain, flank eastern North America, reaching only half the height of its western counterpart. The vast area between the Appalachians and the Rockies includes the glaciated Canadian Shield to the north, the Great Plains in mid-continent, and the Mississippi basin to the south.

South America has more or less the shape of a triangle. The majority of its 17,800,000 sq. km landmass lies close to the equator. Its most important geographical feature is the Andes Mountains, the series of mountain chains that runs uninterrupted from northern Venezuela and Colombia all the way to the island tip of Patagonia. Several mountain peaks reach heights of more than 6,100 metres (m). The highest peak is Aconcagua at almost 7,000 m high.

Depending on the altitude and the amount of rain, South America's vegetation varies. A dense equatorial forest stretches along the Amazon River and its tributaries, surrounded by wide bands of savanna. A semi-arid region in northeastern Brazil is dotted with cactus. Wooded areas are found farther south. Prairies and pampas are common in the lower regions of Uruguay and Argentina; subantarctic forests are found in southern Chile.

The first Europeans to set foot in America were the Vikings who arrived in the tenth century A.D. in Greenland and then, around 1020, in Newfoundland.

# THE DISCOVERY AND SETTLEMENT OF AMERICA

## Who Really Discovered America?

The New World has been discovered at least three times. The most celebrated "discovery" is granted to Christopher Columbus, who landed at San Salvador on October 12, 1492. Columbus called the people of the New World "Indians", because he mistakenly thought he had reached the East Indies. But Columbus was really a latecomer to the New World. Five hundred years earlier, Norsemen, or Vikings, from Greenland had sailed the waters of North America.

The last discovery of America was that of the Spanish expedition led by Christopher Columbus, who arrived in 1492 at the island of San Salvador in the Bahamas.

During the Viking Age, the northern hemisphere was enjoying warm temperatures for the second time since the end of the Pleistocene epoch. Warming seas encouraged Norse explorers to leave traditional coastal routes and strike out across uncharted open water. Some Viking groups ventured westward from their original homes in Scandinavia. By A.D. 870, Norse migrants formed a steady stream into Iceland. Fifty years later, their Icelandic settlements numbered over 30,000 people.

One Viking, Eric the Red, began exploring unknown coastlines even farther west. In doing this, he discovered a harsh, unpopulated land, with plentiful game roaming its mountain valleys. Naming the place "Greenland"—no doubt to enhance the image of his new find—Eric returned to recruit settlers for this new land.

According to a saga of the Greenlanders, one shipload of Icelandic merchants was blown off course to the southwest, where they spied a wooded coastline with low hills. When this ship finally made its way back to Iceland, the son of Eric the Red—young Leif Ericsson—vowed to return to this new-found land. Ericsson did return. About A.D. 1000, he and his crew landed on the eastern coast of North America, which they called Vinland. The Vikings occupied a colony there for about three decades before retreating.

## The Native Americans

The first human footprint on New World soil belongs to aboriginal people—American Indians and the closely related Eskimos. In the Americas, human beings did not evolve from earlier human-like forms. People migrated into this New World as fully evolved *Homo sapiens*.

*Homo sapiens* migrants to America brought with them some basic skills, such as tool-making, flint-chipping, and the means to obtain food, shelter, and clothing. These early immigrants must also have brought with them a basic social organization, as well as beliefs about magic and the supernatural. They certainly also possessed forms of language. When Columbus arrived, Native Americans of Alaska, Canada, and the United States spoke about 2,000 different languages.

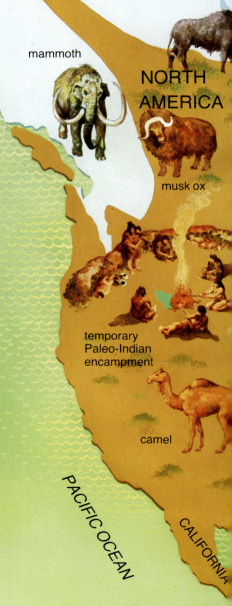

This map shows the western half of North America and the eastern tip of Asia. The white area indicates the extent of penetration by glaciers during periods of glaciation, and the blue area indicates the modified outline of dry land, resulting from a drop in sea level of about 100 metres. By means of this land bridge at some unknown date before 10,000 B.C., the first groups of *Homo sapiens* were able to cross from Asia to Alaska, then to move down through a clear passage between the glaciers towards the middle of the North American continent.

# NORTH AMERICA
## EARLY AMERICANS

The most important event in American history was the passage of the first groups of *Homo sapiens* from Asia into the New World. Nobody knows exactly when, or even where, this happened. Little or nothing is known about the *Homo sapiens* themselves. But evidence from biology, language, and archaeology, convinces scientists that the first Americans came from Asia during the Ice Age.

Scientists do know something about the conditions that permitted this massive migration. During the Pleistocene epoch (or Ice Age), glaciers and mountain ice caps formed simultaneously around the world. Later, during warmer periods, they also melted simultaneously. As the glaciers grew—at times covering all of Canada to a depth of perhaps 3 kilometres—the sea levels dropped as much as 100 metres. The dropping sea levels changed the earth's appearance. The Bering and Chukchi seas retreated to form a land bridge over 2,000 km wide at its maximum. This land bridge allowed east Asians to cross into a new world.

### The Clovis Culture (10,000–9,000 B.C.)

People were established in the New World before 10,000 B.C. The Clovis culture, named after an archaeological site in New Mexico, can be traced from northern Alaska to Guatemala, from the west coast of the United States to the east.

Clovis spear points are among America's most distinctive artifacts. They measure up to 15 centimetres in length and have concave bases with ground-down edges. Clovis people used these spears to hunt big game. Some of the animals, such as the mammoth, camel and long-horned bison, are now extinct due to the change in climate and perhaps also to the hunters' skill.

### Who Were the Oldest Inhabitants?

Clovis people are the first well-documented humans to appear in the Western Hemisphere. Despite much research, there is no positive proof of a pre-Clovis people in North America. Some scholars believe that humans reached North America between 70,000 and 20,000 B.C—long before the Clovis people. They believe that the many different types of spear points dating from between 10,000 and 8000 B.C are evidence of this. Such a variety would be unlikely if the first migration of people had come from Asia only a couple of thousand years earlier.

Stone spear points of the "Clovis" type were characteristic of the first inhabitants of North America.

A group of hunters has succeeded in trapping a mammoth in a marshy area and is attacking it with spears and stones.

As migrating people spread over the New World, they were forced to adapt to many different environments, from interior subarctic to coastal tropical. The cultures that developed within these settlements were also affected by the environmental differences. The variety of both settlements and cultures that existed by about 10,000 B.C. can also be used as evidence that people existed in North America much earlier than this. At Meadowcroft Shelter (near Pittsburgh, Pennsylvania, U.S.A.), archaeologists discovered evidence of a culture that existed from about 17,000 B.C. The oldest stone artifacts appear to date from between 13,000 and 12,000 B.C.

However, the archaeology of Meadowcroft Shelter leaves many questions unanswered. The stone tools found there are few, small, and look just like later artifacts. Also, large animals from the glacial age are missing from Meadowcroft Shelter, and this is surprising for a site so old. The plant remains suggest a mild climate. Yet at times, the ice sheet was less than 75 kilometres to the north.

The two geographical and cultural regions of the southwestern area: California (in brown); the Great Basin, now desert (in violet).

In a region of the Great Basin that is today desert land, one of the ice age lakes is shown in the process of drying up. People gather berries (*left*); a hunter returns with his prey (*centre*); in a cave a group is hard at work chipping stones for tools, working bones, and sewing (*right*). The shape of the cave is modelled on Danger Cave in Utah, U.S.A. The cross section shows the various strata of earth which filled the cave. The lowest level of the cave dates from 9300 B.C.

# THE INTERMOUNTAIN AREA AND THE WEST COAST

## The Paleo-Indians

The oldest inhabitants of North America, also called the Paleo-Indians, rapidly made their way into western North America. They populated both the vast intermountain zone between the Rockies and the Sierra Nevada, and the ranges that face the Pacific Ocean. Paleo-Indians made use of very few resources, depending upon several main food items for survival. In California, the Paleo-Indian people probably hunted now-extinct animals. In the Great Basin, the Paleo-Indians learned to exploit the resources offered by the extensive desert lakes that survived from the Ice Age. Despite environmental difficulties, their stone tools showed remarkable workmanship.

## From Paleo-Indians to Archaic People

With the passage of time, the way of life for these people changed. They became skilled hunters, crafted better tools, and even learned to use wild fruits as a food source. These new, more numerous groups are known as Archaic people. The term *Archaic* indicates the time period during which this life-style dominated. Thanks to their ability to adapt to all kinds of environments, the Archaic people succeeded in effectively populating all of North America.

## The Desert Archaic

Two important ecological shifts define the boundary between Paleo-Indian and Archaic people in the western desert. Gigantic desert lakes began drying up at the end of the Pleistocene epoch. This forced some groups to cluster about the greatly modified shorelines, where they collected bulrush, cattail, and insect larvae, fashioned decoys to hunt waterfowl, and fished during the spawning runs.

Others elected to move to upland mountain valleys. Here they hunted plentiful bighorn sheep or collected herbs. Before about 10,000 B.C., the piñon pine tree grew only along the southern margin of the Great Basin. But about 4500 B.C., it rapidly spread northward, blanketing most of the modern Great Basin. The highly nutritious piñon nut provided a high-bulk food that could be stored for two or three

*Above:* Objects made by Archaic peoples: **1)** abalone shell fishhook; **2)** steatite carving of a killer whale; **3)** two charmstones from central California; **4)** a duck decoy made from marsh reeds.

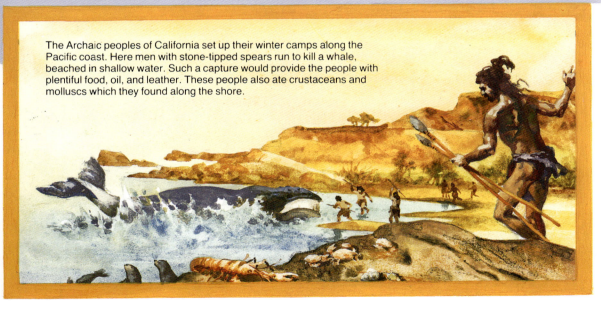

The Archaic peoples of California set up their winter camps along the Pacific coast. Here men with stone-tipped spears run to kill a whale, beached in shallow water. Such a capture would provide the people with plentiful food, oil, and leather. These people also ate crustaceans and molluscs which they found along the shore.

years. The upland desert Archaic people used piñon nuts as their primary staple food whenever a supply was available.

## Archaic Californians

The ten thousand-year-long Archaic period in California is characterized by an economy without agriculture. When big game became extinct, Archaic people continued to hunt smaller animals, but they also relied upon hundreds of plant species for food, medicine, and craft materials. They generally scheduled their movements with the seasons, spending winters at a lower elevation and migrating to higher ground in the springtime. Along the Pacific Coast, seasonal migrations took people from winter camps along the shoreline to summer camps in the interior hills and valleys. The winter camp was often home for several families who joined together in the autumn.

From about 2000 B.C., native Californians began to rely heavily on just a few foods. Valley groups depended mainly on acorns, which were becoming California's most important natural resource. This edible nut could be ground into meal and flour, and stored for long periods of time.

These groups could support large numbers of people by collecting great amounts of certain key resources and storing them for seasons when food was less abundant. Populations were now much larger than during Archaic times. By A.D. 1500, California was home to more than 300,000 Indians, a much greater number than in any comparable area north of Mexico.

This map shows the northwestern region. The coast is in blue; the interior plateau is in yellow.

A group of coastal Indians navigates an ocean-going canoe. Hollowed out from a single tree trunk, the canoe is about 20 metres long.

# THE NORTHWEST COAST

America's Northwest Coast extends along the Pacific Ocean from Yakutat Bay in southern Alaska to the Humboldt Bay in northern California. This coastline is cut by a network of channels and fjords, with thousands of islands, large and small. The warm Japanese Current, which flows south along the coast from Alaska, creates a moderate climate with heavy rainfall.

The earliest human remains from southeastern Alaska, British Columbia, Washington, and Oregon show no major differences between coastal and interior communities. But such differences developed through time, leading to rather different adaptations. While hunters and river fishers populated the inland, the groups settled along the Northwest Coast underwent rapid development. Although agriculture was never practised here and ceramics were unknown, Northwest Coast peoples are well known for their large numbers, rich ceremonies, and for the importance they attached to property, rank, and personal pride.

## The Way of Life Changes

On the Northwest Coast, population increased greatly between 2000 and 1000 B.C. Sometime thereafter there emerged a single culture, which was adapted along the coast both by people to the north and to the south. This way of life made use of marine resources and relied on a mountainous interior rich in fish and game to achieve the "culture of abundance" that so impressed the earliest European explorers of Northwest America.

Large villages were invariably located at the water's edge on a beach convenient for landing canoes. However, traces of smaller, special-purpose sites also remain. In the north, houses were nearly square and between 10 and 20 metres across. They also had vertical side planking and gabled roofs. Sometimes a house had terraced sides, with the cooking fire located on the lower level and sleeping areas on the upper levels. In the south, houses were long and narrow, and occupied by several families, each with its own fire. One such house was nearly 150 metres long and 20 metres wide. Large wooden houses have been constructed on the Northwest Coast for more than 3,000 years.

Artifacts became increasingly diverse, particularly after 1500 B.C. Stone artifacts such as cutting tools and bowls became common. Bone, shell, and wooden tools were abundant. Woodworking was highly developed on the Northwest Coast; houses, canoes, bowls, spoons, boxes, drums, and masks were decorated with symbolic and artistic patterns.

wooden sculpture

*Right:* A circular pithouse, with a central fireplace, is half buried in the ground. Its tent-like roof is supported by poles and completed with matting. Two women are pounding cereals in a stone mortar, while some men have tanned skins and are stretching them out to dry.

The ground plan (*left*) and cross section (*immediately below*) show the detail of a half-buried dwelling at Surprise Valley between 4000 and 3000 B.C. The holes left by the poles and the location of the central fireplace can be seen on the ground plan. The cross section shows the entrance ramp.

## Life on the Plateaus of the Interior

A hunting tradition developed on the interior plateaus by at least 8000 B.C. Elk, deer, antelope, beavers, rabbits, and rodents were favourite prey. Two thousand years later, this list broadened to include salmon and river molluscs such as mussels and clams. Most sites cluster near major rivers, and there is little evidence of upland exploitation.

The interior people—those living away from the coasts—began to live in villages of deeply excavated houses called pithouses. Some of these exceeded 20 metres in diameter. As many as 25 people could winter in one house. With a central fireplace, these houses were roofed with bark or woven matting.

Interior people created thousands of stone carvings called petroglyphs. Even today, many cliff faces and boulders are covered with drawings of people, mountain sheep, deer, elk, salmon, beavers, and imaginary animals. Some petroglyphs tell a story while others seem to be connected with death rites, and a few appear to be tribal symbols.

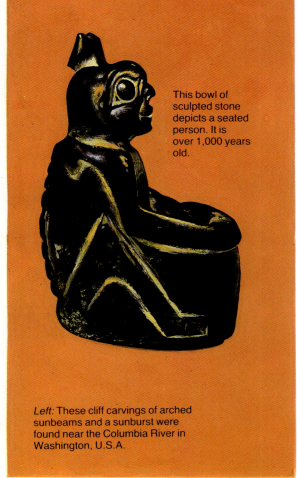

This bowl of sculpted stone depicts a seated person. It is over 1,000 years old.

*Left:* These cliff carvings of arched sunbeams and a sunburst were found near the Columbia River in Washington, U.S.A.

11

# ANCIENT PEOPLE AND EARLY FARMERS IN THE AMERICAN SOUTHWEST

## Paleo-Indians and Archaic (Desert) People

The earliest human inhabitants of the Southwest were Paleo-Indians of the late Pleistocene epoch (10,000 to 15,000 years ago). They were skilled hunters and lived off now-extinct species of elephant, bison, camel, and horse that roamed the region during that cool, wet period.

The shift towards a warm, dry climate, much like that of the present-day Southwest, began about 9,000 years ago. This shift caused dramatic changes in animal and plant populations. The people who adapted to these conditions were the Archaic or Desert people. These people relied on harvesting wild plants and hunting small animals. A variety of cultural artifacts recovered from dry caves throughout the Southwest testify to their skill in textile and basketry crafts. About 2,000 years ago, some Desert people of southern Arizona and New Mexico began growing maize, beans, and squash.

## Early Agriculture

Many early farming cultures have been identified in the Southwest. The best known of these are the Hohokam (of the low deserts of south-central Arizona), the mountain-dwelling Mogollon (of central and southern Arizona and New Mexico), and the Anasazi (of the Four Corners region that includes northwestern New Mexico, southwestern Colorado, southeastern Utah, and northeastern Arizona). None of these people had domestic animals other than dogs and turkeys, nor did any have a written language. Knowledge of them comes mainly through archaeological exploration.

## The Hohokam

The best-known Hohokam village is called Snaketown, located near the modern city of Phoenix in Arizona, U.S.A. It may have been occupied as early as 300 B.C. and abandoned about A.D. 1300. Excavations there document the evolution of Hohokam society. Archaeologists organize this society into four major periods called the Pioneer period (about 300 B.C.-A.D. 500), the Colonial period (about A.D. 500-900), the Sedentary period (about A.D. 900-1100), and the Classic period (about A.D. 1100-1500).

Pioneer people lived in small villages of wattle and daub houses and built irrigation canals to water their fields in the low desert country. Weaving, pottery, and shell jewellery were important household crafts. During the Colonial period, populations increased and new communities were established in the mountains and plateaus of central and eastern Arizona. Hohokam society became more complex and crafts more sophisticated. During the Sedentary and Classic periods, villages became larger, but Hohokam territory shrank. In some Classic period communities, thick-walled, multi-storey adobe (mud) houses were built, and high walls surrounded the villages.

Hohokam ritual architecture included large community houses, ball courts similar to those

*Left, above:* A reconstruction of the Hohokam settlement in Casagrande, Arizona. The building of the settlement is made of bricks of hardened earth and wood. It required the excavation of massive amounts of earth and the transportation of timber from mountains over 80 kilometres away.

**1)** A piece of Hohokam pottery found in Snaketown, Arizona, 1000-1100 B.C. **2)** This drawing of a turkey was taken from a piece of Mimbres pottery that dates from A.D. 1100-1300. The turkey and the dog were the only domesticated animals. **3)** A splendid example of Mimbres pottery.

*Left, below:* The life of the Hohokam people was based on agriculture, especially on maize cultivation, which was made possible by an effective system of irrigation.

A group of Hohokam works with crude tools to maintain a canal that brings water for irrigation from mountains to fields.

found throughout Central America and truncated pyramids used as dance plazas or as temple platforms. Other evidence of contact between the Hohokam and the cultures of Mexico include pyrite mirrors and copper bells found at Hohokam sites.

## The Mogollon

The Mogollon people of the mountains and deserts of southern New Mexico and Arizona are thought to be descended from Desert people who had lived in the region for thousands of years. They lived in a varied environment, and display a variety of adaptations. Generally, their small villages contained pithouses, and their pottery was usually unpainted redware.

Several major Mogollon subgroups have been described. The best known of these is the Mimbres branch of southwestern New Mexico who made remarkable black-and-white painted pottery that was ritually "killed" and buried with their dead. Strong Anasazi influences affected northern Mogollon peoples after about A.D. 1050, and for reasons not well understood, most Mogollon villages were abandoned and the people scattered.

# THE ANASAZI

The Anasazi are among the best-known prehistoric southwestern cultures. The name comes from a Navajo Indian word meaning "the Ancient Ones," and actually describes a successful way of life that was shared by many different peoples. The modern Pueblo Indian tribes of the southwestern United States are descendants of the Anasazi. Their history is subdivided into the following periods (and approximate dates): Basketmaker (A.D. 200-700), Pueblo I and Pueblo II (A.D. 700-1050), Pueblo III (A.D. 1050-1300), Pueblo IV (A.D. 1300-1700), and Pueblo V (A.D. 1700-the present).

## Early Pueblo Life

The period from Basketmaker to Pueblo II saw a gradual evolution of the Anasazi way of life. Basketmaker people cultivated maize, beans, and squash, hunted, and gathered wild vegetables. Their white or grey pottery was often decorated with black paint. Early Basketmaker people lived in the Rio Grande Valley. Their pithouses resembled those of the Mogollon people.

Pueblo I and Pueblo II people built above-ground houses with connecting rooms. South-facing rock shelters in narrow canyons were favourite building sites. Because ceremony was important, most villages were built around a dance plaza and ritual structures called kivas which resembled old-style pithouses. Pottery decoration became more complex, and regional styles developed. The bow and arrow and loom-woven cotton textiles were introduced.

## The Classic Pueblo Period

By the time of the Pueblo III, or Classic Pueblo period, the Anasazi dwellings had taken on the familiar pueblo look. During this period, the village populations increased, although actual territory decreased as people moved into the huge pueblo structures. Some of these had hundreds of connecting rooms.

Some pueblos, such as the one in Mesa Verde, Arizona, were great houses built on cliffs. Others were huge, apartment-like structures like that of the Chaco Canyon. This narrow, dry valley became an early centre for Pueblo III culture. Roads terminated there, linking it to about a hundred separate communities, each built in the unique Chacoan architectural style. That style is characterized by fine masonry used to build houses that were several storeys high. These houses were terraced to catch the warmth of the sun.

Pueblo Bonito at Chaco Canyon with more than 800 rooms was the largest of the Chaco great houses. Built in three major stages between about A.D. 950 and 1130, it still stands four storeys high and may once have had a fifth level. Within 15 kilometres of it are a dozen similar buildings as well as many smaller villages. Together, these may have housed as many as 6,000 people.

Chaco Canyon appears to have been the centre of a complex economic, ritual, and political system. But for reasons that are unclear, the Chaco system ended in about A.D. 1150. During the remainder of the Pueblo III era, Anasazi culture was based in the less dry Mesa Verde area. During the 1200s and 1300s, the Anasazi moved into the Rio Grande Valley.

## The Late Prehistoric Period

The collapse of the Chaco system was among the first of many such events during the two centuries following A.D. 1150. By the time the first Europeans arrived in the 1530s, the Anasazi people had gained new stability. As many as 50,000 to 100,000 Anasazi people (called Pueblos by the Spanish explorers) were living in more than a hundred towns and smaller villages in New Mexico and Arizona.

All the Anasazi towns and villages had similar economic, political, social, and ritual systems, but the people spoke at least six different languages. They formed loose alliances with one another but were organized as independent yet equal communities based on farming. Their governments were *theocratic*, which means that the people believed their leaders to be divinely guided, but all community members were active in ritual life.

Most Pueblo villages were of multi-storey, terraced buildings with hundreds of rooms arranged around plazas. Although they had settled in a new territory, these late Anasazi people were still much like their ancestors.

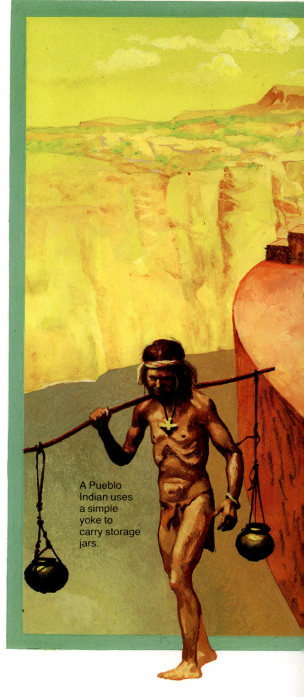

A Pueblo Indian uses a simple yoke to carry storage jars.

*Large-scale view, above:* This reconstruction shows the centre of Pueblo Bonito as it must have appeared about A.D. 1000. The scale is imposing: dwellings are arranged on four levels around the outer wall; all the circular structures with access ladders in the middle indicate the presence of a kiva or ceremonial room.

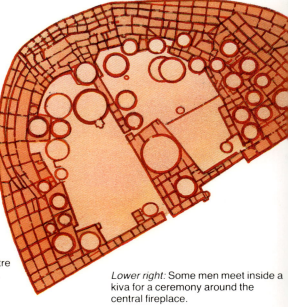

A plan of the centre of Pueblo Bonito.

*Lower right:* Some men meet inside a kiva for a ceremony around the central fireplace.

This map shows the Great Plains region marked in green.

# THE GREAT PLAINS

The Great Plains of North America occupy roughly 2,600,000 square kilometres. The Plains are a flat grassland of cold winters, hot summers, and sparse, unpredictable rainfall. Trees occur only near streams, on hilly slopes, and on low mountains.

## Early Big-Game Hunters (10,000-5000 B.C.)

The oldest proof that Plains people's lives centred on hunting animals comes from mammoth kill sites, most dating between about 9500 B.C. and 9000 B.C. At these sites, archaeologists have found Clovis spear points, cutting tools, a variety of bone tools, and milling stones.

At the end of the Pleistocene epoch, conifer forests in the Great Plains area were gradually replaced by deciduous forests. Between 8000 and 6000 B.C., all forest was replaced by grassland. Thus, about ten thousand years ago, large portions of the Great Plains became suitable for large herbivores. From this time on, bison provided the material and spiritual focus for human life on the American Plains.

## The Plains Archaic People and the Transformation of the Plains (5000 B.C.-A.D. 900)

The Plains Archaic people lived by a cycle of

A woman works the soil with a hoe made from the shoulder blade of a bison. *(See detailed drawing on the right.)*

A hunter hurls his spear using a spear-thrower. This simple device "lengthened" the arm, and so increased the force and the range of the throw. *(See detailed drawing above.)*

Archaic hunters drive bison into a trap consisting of a stockade built at the base of a cliff.

hunting small game and gathering seeds, tubers, nuts, berries, and other foods. But whenever possible, the Plains Archaic people hunted bison. Eventually, the Great Plains people shifted from general big-game hunting to exclusive bison hunting. Until the introduction of farming, it was the presence of bison that allowed the human population to grow.

The Archaic life-style continued into the final centuries B.C.. Over this great stretch of time, many local differences arose among the people. Pottery making was introduced to the Plains, as was the building of mounds and earth fortresses. Such sites are scattered across the Plains but seem to diminish westwards towards the Rockies.

Simple hunting and gathering provided sustenance in most sites. Bone refuse found at sites in the central Plains suggests that deer and small mammals were more important prey than bison at this time. But bison hunting remained important to the north and west. Maize cultivation was typical of the Hopewellian communities near present-day Kansas City and perhaps in Nebraska as well.

## The Plains Villages (A.D. 900 and Later)

In the eastern Plains (from North Dakota to northern Texas) and in the western Plains (from Montana to New Mexico), village life developed around agriculture. This culture depended on maize and other cultivated plants. Villages following this tradition worked the rich soils of the Missouri River and its tributaries with hoes made of bison bones. Despite this farming tradition, people along the eastern Plains continued to depend on wild plant foods and animals (including bison) for a major portion of their diet. An agricultural economy in the drought-prone central Plains was hazardous. Bison remained a more reliable food source.

Many eastern Plains villages were fortified with dry moats and stockades. Most sites show evidence of large, well-built lodges used by several families and a number of underground storage pits. Usually, the people lived here all year round. In the west, Plains groups mixed with the Puebloan people of the Southwest and adopted some of their practices.

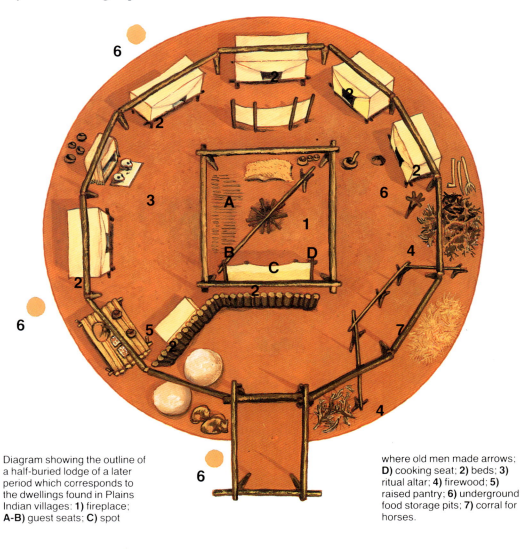

Diagram showing the outline of a half-buried lodge of a later period which corresponds to the dwellings found in Plains Indian villages: **1)** fireplace; **A-B)** guest seats; **C)** spot where old men made arrows; **D)** cooking seat; **2)** beds; **3)** ritual altar; **4)** firewood; **5)** raised pantry; **6)** underground food storage pits; **7)** corral for horses.

The Southeast region is shown in blue on the map.

A group of nomads in the woods of the Northeast. Their food comes from hunting and gathering wild fruits.

*Right:* Several objects characteristic of the Archaic people: **1)** a needle, a hook, and a small bone pipe; **2)** a stone arrowhead; **3)** two stone axes.

# PEOPLES OF THE SOUTHEAST REGIONS

The American Southeast includes the coastal plain and the southern half of the Appalachian Mountains. But Southeastern cultural history centres on major river valleys—especially those of the Tennessee and Mississippi rivers. For it was here that the most complex Native American social and political organizations north of Mexico developed.

## The Paleo-Indian Tradition (10,000-6000 B.C.)

The group that first occupied the southeast regions are known as the Paleo-Indians. This term identifies a simple people who fashioned stone tools much like those of their contemporaries on the Great Plains. But life for the east Paleo-Indian peoples probably differed greatly from the big-game hunting pattern evident on the Plains. In particular, the eastern Paleo-Indians concentrated their efforts on river valley resources.

## The Southeastern Archaic People (6000-700 B.C.)

The Archaic population was generally spread across the southeastern landscape in small bands. The small numbers allowed each group to react quickly to local variations in food resources. The Archaic people's ability to adapt protected them against the failure of any particular plant or animal species.

This adaptability was lost, however, when population increases reduced food resources. Later Archaic sites indicate that people were trying to develop a new economic system in order to deal with the year-to-year swings in supplies. The people were particularly interested in improving the exchange, distribution, and storage of goods.

The earliest pottery in North America also appears in the Southeast about this time. In the lower Mississippi Valley, people began constructing earthworks, huge mounds of earth. One such earthwork was called Poverty Point. It was built in Louisiana about 1300 B.C. At the site there is a large bird-shaped earthen mound nearly 23 metres high. Not far away is an earthwork of six circular ridges. The largest

The Sedentary period saw the first attempts to domesticate plants, such as sunflowers, gourds, and goosefoot, in areas with an abundant water supply.

The Poverty Point complex is one of the most imposing structures of American prehistory. Notice the mound in the shape of a bird in the upper right corner and the six concentric ridges of the earthworks.

These small blocks of fired clay were probably heated in the fireplace and then tossed into pots of water for cooking food.

This is an example of the oldest terra-cotta pottery in the Southeast. It is simple in form and made from a mixture of clay and vegetable fibres.

Burial among the Archaic Plains Indians, as found at Indian Knoll, Kentucky. Great numbers of such graves exist. The dead person was placed in this characteristic crouched position.

of these is almost 1,200 metres across. These ridges were probably used as dwellings.

The Poverty Point complex is a mystery. The massive earthworks found there suggest that this site was a major ceremonial area. It was densely populated and an economic centre. Whatever the cultural basis, Poverty Point was abandoned. Nearly a thousand years passed before the Southeast again saw such elaborate ceremonial organization.

## The Sedentary Period (700 B.C.–A.D. 700)

The use of ceramics spread throughout eastern North America shortly after 700 B.C. The introduction of ceramics probably did not bring great changes to the southeast people. But the rapid spread of the craft indicates that settlements had become permanent. The building of mounds and fortresses also became important at this time. Although both structures already existed, many more were built during the Sedentary period. This increase also suggests that settlements had become more permanent.

During the Sedentary period, long-distance trade began. As this method of exchange became popular, trade networks affected most of eastern North America. This exchange process also encouraged the people to expand their resources. The Sedentary period peoples learned to grow native plants such as sunflower, goosefoot (*Chenopodium*), and other river bottom plants. Farming these plants provided the southeastern people with the broader resource base they needed.

# THE NORTHEAST WOODLAND

## The Eastern Paleo-Indian Tradition (9000-8000 B.C.)

Meadowcroft Shelter is the oldest, well-documented archaeological site in North America. Yet in the prehistory of the Northeast region, Meadowcroft remains unique. Elsewhere there is widespread evidence of hunters using fluted-point spears. These hunters had apparently moved in from the south. By 10,000 B.C., the plant and animal life in the Ohio Valley and farther north into Wisconsin, Michigan, and Ontario was plentiful enough to support scattered bands of hunters. The tool forms found throughout the Northeast were all very similar. The widespread similarity suggests that a basic toolmaking ability may have been adapted to a wide variety of environments, from coastal plain to upland, from river valley to north lakes. Animal bones found in association with these early fluted points are usually of woodland caribou, although bones of rodents, deer, and elk are also present.

## The Northeastern Archaic People (8000-1000 B.C.)

The Archaic life-style did not spread from a single centre. Rather, this culture appears to have evolved locally at the end of the glacier periods. Existence in the Northeast depended on hunting, fishing, and plant-gathering. The people used large, broad-bladed arrow heads and polished-bone tools.

After 4000 B.C., these populations developed a distinctive method of working copper. Large and abundant copper nuggets were found on the surface of rock outcrops and in glacial deposits, especially in the Lake Superior area. These nuggets were worked by cold- and hot-hammering methods into spears, knives, adzes, gouges, awls, and fishhooks.

## The Adena Culture (1000 B.C.)

The Adena culture flourished in present-day Ohio about 1000 B.C. The Adena people are known to have been skilled in pottery-making and other crafts. Their sites also show that they experimented in agriculture but depended on hunting, fishing, and gathering.

The Adena culture is best known for its mound building. The Adena burial mounds were usually cone-shaped. One of the largest known mounds, Grave Creek Mound in West Virginia, is 20 metres high. The mounds were usually simple graves of dirt, stone, and other materials heaped over the dead. But some tombs, such as those of the leaders, were built of timber. These tombs also contained grave goods, or gifts to the dead, such as stone tools.

Around the mounds, the Adena people often built huge enclosures, or embankments. These enclosures were also mounds, and they were often perfectly circular in shape. Some, however, were shaped like animals. The one shown opposite is shaped like a snake and is called the Great Serpent Mound. Although some embankments contained graves, they were mainly used for ceremonies.

## Hopewell Culture (300 B.C.-A.D. 200)

The Hopewell culture, which followed the Adena, is also known for its complex burial mounds, particularly in central Ohio, U.S.A. Their sites have many more mounds than the Adena's, but these too are surrounded by embankments. Some of the huge earthworks may have been used for defence, but most were used in ceremonies or as burial mounds.

Hopewell tombs were made of wood, as in Adena, although they were more complex and had a series of rooms. Grave goods were more plentiful in these tombs because the Hopewell believed the dead would need things in the next world. Gifts to the dead included ornaments of polished stone or metal, jewellery, pipes, engraved bones, flints, and weapons. The Hopewell sometimes cremated their dead. The bodies were cremated in clay-lined pits, and the ashes were placed in the tombs.

The Hopewell were also skilled in crafts. Copperwork flourished, and small amounts of beaten gold and silver have also been found. Hopewell pottery is mostly decorated with cord marks, made when the clay was still wet.

On the map, the yellow indicates the Northeast region.

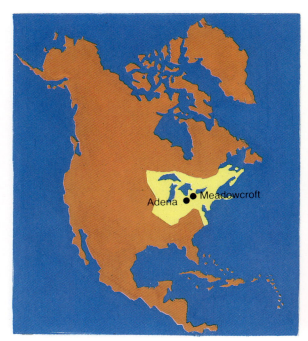

A cutaway view of the dwelling of the Adena people shows the interior and the fireplace. The reconstruction is based on excavations at Cowan Creek, Ohio.

Two objects from the Adena culture are shown. 1) The pattern on this terra-cotta vase has been cut into the clay. 2) This stone-sculptured pipe is an excellent example of Adena skill. The tobacco was placed in the pipe bowl behind the legs. A hole for the pipe stem was on top of the head.

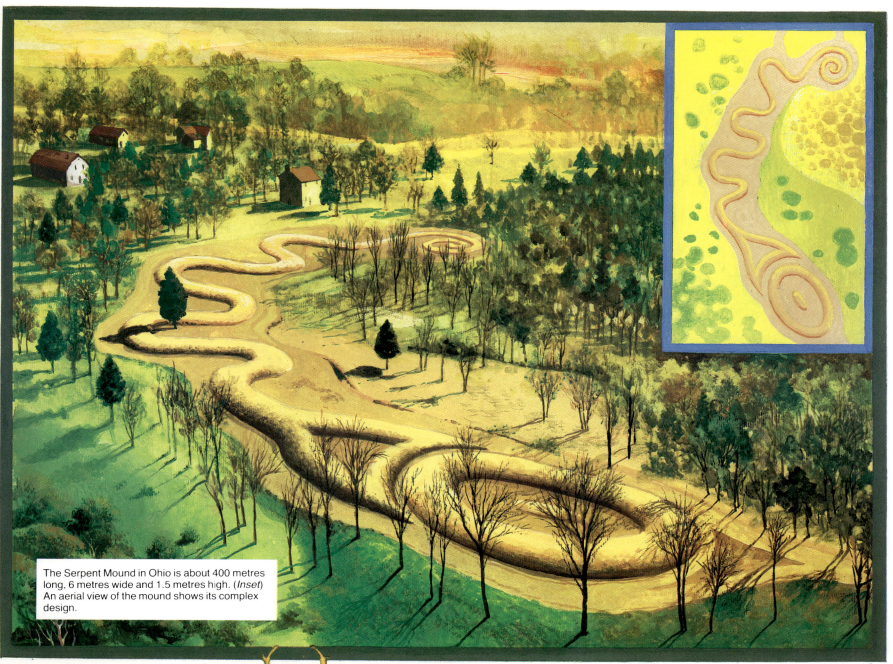

The Serpent Mound in Ohio is about 400 metres long, 6 metres wide and 1.5 metres high. (*Inset*) An aerial view of the mound shows its complex design.

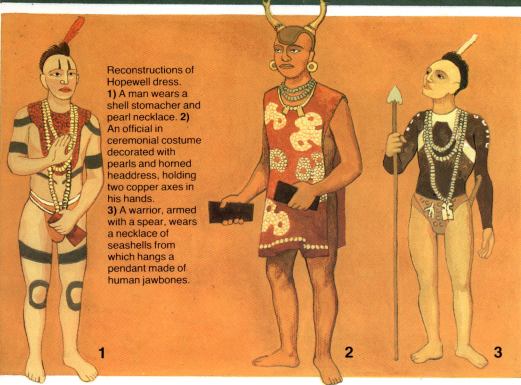

Reconstructions of Hopewell dress.
**1)** A man wears a shell stomacher and pearl necklace. **2)** An official in ceremonial costume decorated with pearls and horned headdress, holding two copper axes in his hands.
**3)** A warrior, armed with a spear, wears a necklace of seashells from which hangs a pendant made of human jawbones.

A Hopewell carved stone pipe in the shape of a bird. The mouthpiece is on the left; the pipe bowl is in the bird's back.

A decorated terra-cotta pot.

# THE MISSISSIPPIAN PEOPLE

## The Eastern Regions in the Late Prehistoric Period (A.D. 700-1540)

Throughout much of the eastern United States, the Late Prehistoric period is characterized by increased dependence upon agricultural products.

The term *Mississippian* describes the highly complex Late Prehistoric societies that thrived along major river valleys of the eastern United States. People living along the Tennessee, Cumberland, and Mississippi rivers made huge earth mounds, and pottery with crushed shells added to temper the clay. Much of the Northeast cultures did not develop in the same way, although people there did achieve some dependence upon agriculture.

## Agriculture and the Mississippian Settlements

Agriculture for Mississippian peoples was vastly different from that practised by European farmers. Because Native Americans lacked domesticated draught animals, agriculture was restricted to hoe cultivation of light soils. Mississippian agriculture was therefore largely restricted to fertile river valleys.

As people became more agricultural, centralized authorities became more important. And the more centralized the authorities, and the more organized the people became, the more agriculture became essential for survival.

Mississippian settlements were organized into a specialized social hierarchy. Large, centralized sites with many platform-type mounds functioned as administrative centres. A hierarchy of bureaucrats and priests—including community chiefs, war chiefs, mortuary priests, and clan heads—supervised the production, collection, and distribution of foods and materials. They also presided over the city, and the construction of mounds and fortifications.

Typical Mississippian towns were planned settlements, with rectangular, single-family houses arranged around an open, central square. The town meeting house, chief's house, and a charnel house were built on adjacent earthen platform mounds. Round about were smaller villages, farm buildings, hunting or fishing zones, and quarries.

## The Southern Cult

In the Late Prehistoric period a variety of ritual ceremonies were performed. These rites were intended to honour ancestors, celebrate successful harvest, hunts and warfare, and accompany the burial of important leaders.

During the Mississippian period, a special type of cult formed over much of the East. Archaeological evidence of this cult is provided by various objects that began to appear about A.D. 1000, reaching a peak between 1200 and 1400. Called the Southern Cult, this huge network was concentrated in three regions: Moundville (Alabama), Etowah (Georgia), and Spiro (Oklahoma). However, the distribution of Southern Cult objects extended beyond the limits of any single Mississippian cultural complex. In addition to small, luxury items, it seems that Southern Cult exchange may have involved subsistence resources such as food. Evidence suggests that the Southern Cult's influence may have extended into the Southeast.

## The Decline of the Mississippians

Many of the great Mississippian centres were thriving when the Spaniard De Soto first came to the American Southeast in A.D. 1540. The decline of these Late Prehistoric societies was directly related to European incursions into their territory.

*Opposite page, centre:* The Mississippian settlement at Kincaid, Illinois, was built along the river and included temples, palaces, living quarters, fields, and woods (which provided the people with timber, game, and wild berries).

*Opposite page, at top:* **1)** A monolithic axe of polished stone comes from Moundville, Alabama. **2)** This cup's handle is shaped like a crested duck. **3)** This vessel is in the shape of a human head. *Drawings 5-10:* Representations of animal-gods from the southern cult reflect a high level of skill on the part of the artisans who etched them on copper (**4**).

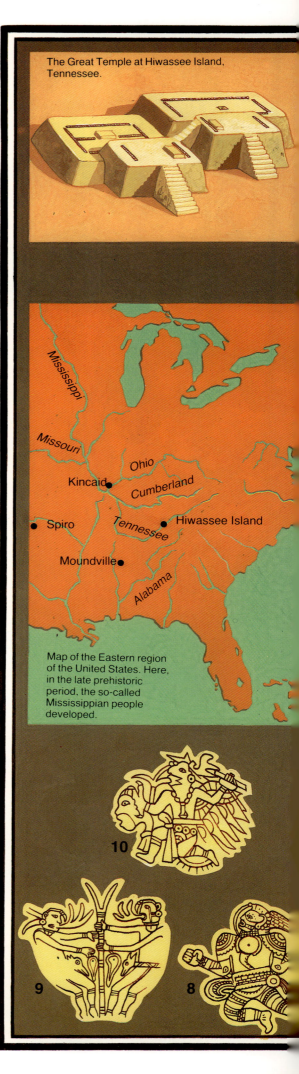

The Great Temple at Hiwassee Island, Tennessee.

Map of the Eastern region of the United States. Here, in the late prehistoric period, the so-called Mississippian people developed.

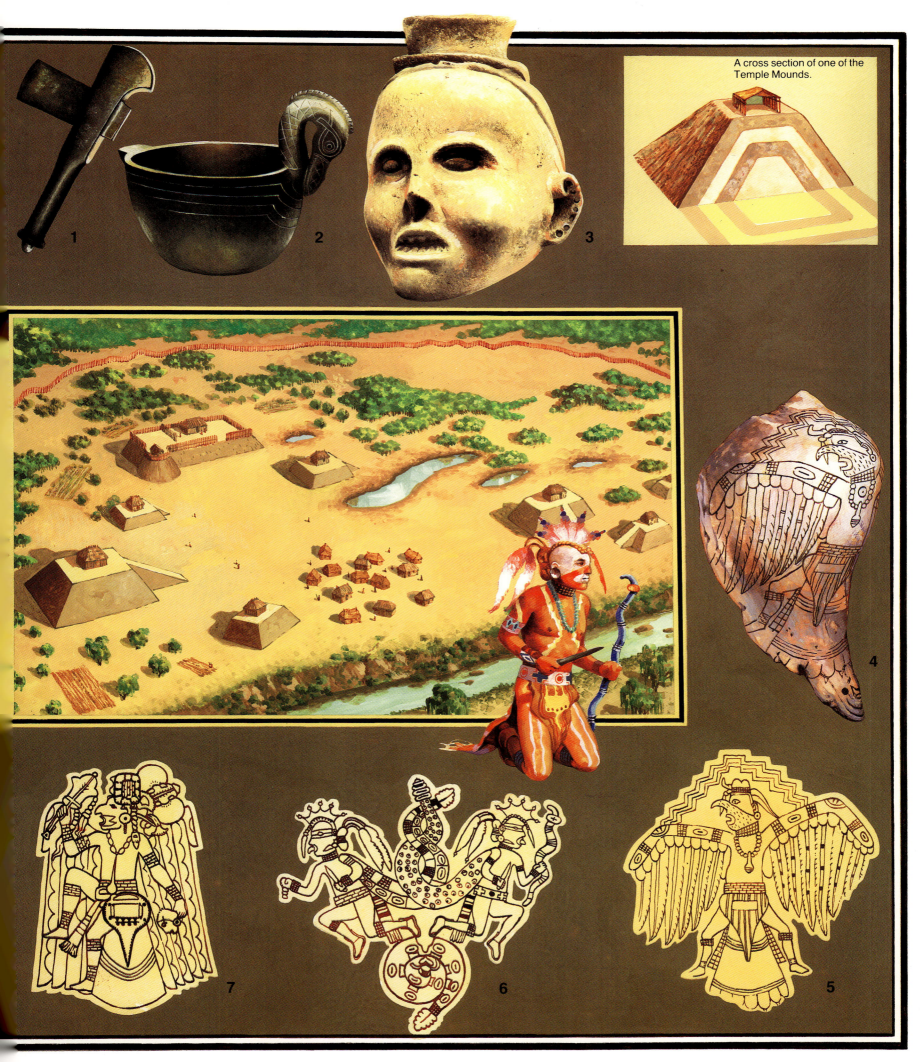

A cross section of one of the Temple Mounds.

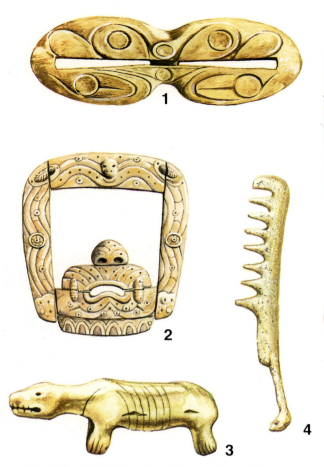

Ivory artifacts from the Ipiutak culture: **1)** snow glasses; **2)** a sculpture in the form of a mask; **3)** polar bear; **4)** instrument of unknown use, possibly a comb; **5)** spear point with stone blades attached.

# THE ARCTIC

The Arctic is a vast, cold, treeless zone. Long before Europeans penetrated this harsh land, the Arctic had been successfully occupied by Native Americans. Often called Eskimo, they call themselves Inuit, meaning simply "the people." Only the Inuit achieved a successful, year-round adaptation to Arctic conditions without agriculture and domestic animals. Permanent human presence came later in the Arctic than in most other areas of the world.

## The Northern Archaic People (4000-2400 B.C.)

The oldest evidence of human occupation dates from between 7000 and 5000 B.C. After about 4000 B.C., the warming climate had stimulated the complete forestation of the Alaskan interior. This resulted in a northward shift of the northern edge of the Canadian forest. These new forests were inhabited by Archaic people. Subsistence methods were similar to those used in more southerly parts of forested continental America. The most important game was caribou. Moose and smaller animals, however, were also hunted.

In central Canada, a similar northward movement had begun by about 6000 B.C., bringing caribou hunters north as they followed the shifting treeline.

## The Ancestors of the Inuit (2000-1000 B.C.)

Arctic people of the so-called Small Tool tradition lived mostly inland, hunting caribou and occasionally visiting the coast to take seals. Surprisingly, there is no solid evidence that at this early date these people hunted seals by cutting holes through the ice—a technique considered indispensable for hunters living permanently on the Arctic coast. These people apparently also lacked boats and dogs. They were the ancestors of modern Inuit people.

Great skill was required to make a bone harpoon: **1)** assembled harpoon, **2)** head, **3)** flexible joint linking head to shaft, **4)** fastener to hold line to shaft, **5)** overall harpoon assembly and **6)** details of harpoon head.

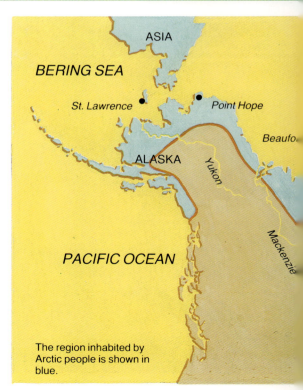

The region inhabited by Arctic people is shown in blue.

The hunter sometimes attached inflatable sealskin floats to the end of the harpoon line. The floats and the attached iron ring, which acted as a brake, prevented the seal from escaping beneath the ice.

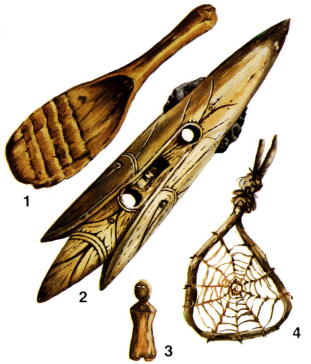

An outside view and a cross section show the details of an igloo or snow-block house. The entrance to the igloo is through a narrow tunnel.

Shown here are artifacts from the Thule culture: **1)** wooden spatula, **2)** harpoon head made from walrus tusk with flint blade inserts, **3)** doll made from bark, **4)** whalebone ladle, and **5)** terra-cotta lamp.

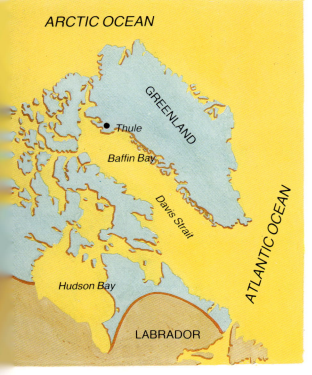

## The Conquest of the Arctic Coast (1000 B.C.–A.D. 1000)

After a period of apparent depopulation, new groups appeared in the Arctic. In the early years A.D., one of these groups had developed a distinctive culture of its own. The Ipiutak culture lasted more than 500 years. One burial site shows that up to 4,000 people lived there in 800 log-and-turf houses. Ipiutak people hunted walrus and seal from early spring through the summer. In the winter, they moved inland and hunted caribou.

Shallow Ipiutak graves contained small sculptures of walruses, bears, and imaginary animals. Excavations have also turned up fine ivory objects carved in spirals and linked chains. From walrus tusks, the Ipiutak carved harpoon points. From walrus hide they made a line that was the strongest line known before the invention of the steel cable.

## The Thule Tradition (100–1800 A.D.)

Sometime around A.D. 1100, the Thule people—immediate ancestors of modern Inuit—spread rapidly throughout northern Canada and Greenland. This was probably due to warmer weather, which changed the path of sea mammal migration. These were the first Americans to make contact with Europeans when the Norsemen arrived in Greenland in A.D. 985.

The subarctic region, shown in yellow, corresponds to the central belt of present-day Canada.

A cliff painting discovered in Ontario, Canada, depicts men and spotted deer.

# THE PEOPLE OF THE SUBARCTIC

Extreme northeastern North America was the "newest" land surface in the New World. It was the last to emerge from beneath the glaciers. Tundra flora rapidly moved into the newly liberated landscape, and various animal species were then drawn into these warmer ecosystems. People did not move into the area until centuries later.

Today, the treeline separating the Arctic from subarctic provides a broad transitional zone. This zone includes tundra and boreal forest. The forested portion is almost impenetrable. Winters in the boreal forest and the tundra are similar. However, summers in the forest are longer and warmer.

## The Northern Archaic Period

The first recognizable human activity in the subarctic occurred during the Paleo-Indian period. As the forests shifted farther north, a forest barrier formed between the tundra and the temperate grasslands. That meant that people had various environments in which to live. In this period of continuous change, there emerged a generalized capability to adapt to forest life. This is the so-called Northern Archaic period.

Caribou hunting remained the primary economic activity on the northern fringes of the forest. To the south, moose and deer were the main prey animals.

During this period, human populations slowly expanded. The number of permanent settlements increased. As groups moved from place to place less often, technological capacities improved.

Caribou hunters, wearing animal skins and antlers to camouflage themselves, approach a group of caribou.

A subarctic hunter uses a bow-drill made from caribou antlers. The rotary motion of the point is produced by vigorously bowing the drill, so that the cord rotates the shaft.

A cliff painting in Ontario, Canada, depicts a moose, some men in a canoe, and a horned water snake.

Groups of caribou hunters settled in the area around Hudson Bay. Many caribou-hunting sites have been found along the rivers and lakes that lay across the migratory paths of the herds.

The stone implements found in these sites were designed for hunting and killing, skinning and butchering, cutting and splitting bone, and scraping and softening hides. They were also useful in the manufacture of other caribou-related products.

A cold spell hit the region in about 1500 B.C., causing the treeline to shift to the south. Unable to cope with increasingly difficult winter conditions, Archaic people had no choice but to retreat southward. The vacuum left by their withdrawal did not last long, since this same cold period stimulated an expansion of arctic hunters into the interior barren lands.

## The People of the North Atlantic Coast (4500-1500 B.C.)

During this period, groups of people came to inhabit the Atlantic shores from Labrador to Maine. Many of their archaeological sites are located near deep ocean waters rich in marine species, especially seals and small whales. Artifacts there show that people hunted marine animals. Also, they were skilled boatbuilders and sailors. Because this marine focus was seasonal, the people also depended on land hunting.

These people flourished during the first major warm period following the glaciations. Their success waned when the cooler conditions set in about 1500 B.C.

# MESOAMERICA
## EARLY INHABITANTS

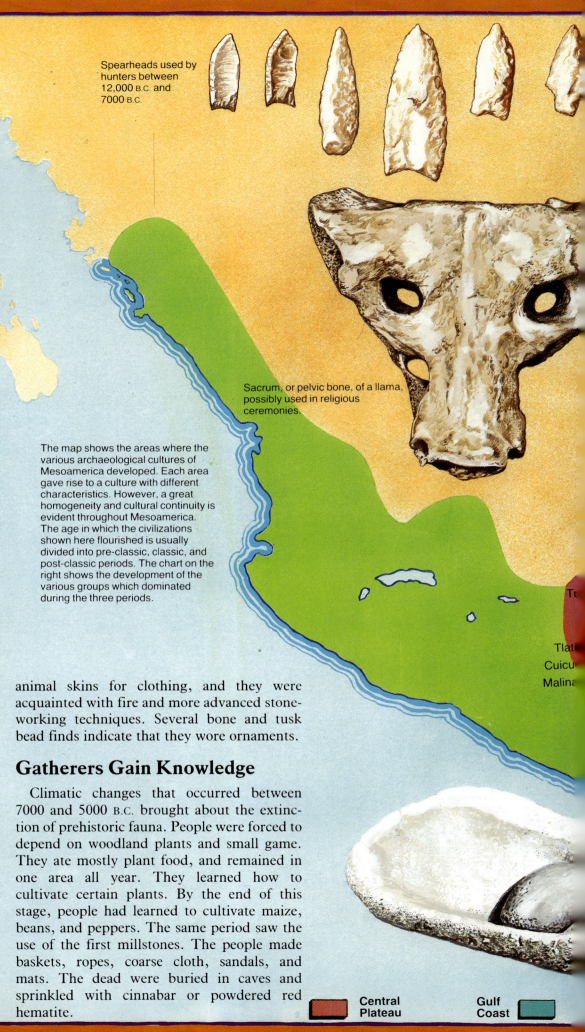

Spearheads used by hunters between 12,000 B.C. and 7000 B.C.

Sacrum, or pelvic bone, of a llama, possibly used in religious ceremonies.

The map shows the areas where the various archaeological cultures of Mesoamerica developed. Each area gave rise to a culture with different characteristics. However, a great homogeneity and cultural continuity is evident throughout Mesoamerica. The age in which the civilizations shown here flourished is usually divided into pre-classic, classic, and post-classic periods. The chart on the right shows the development of the various groups which dominated during the three periods.

**Central Plateau**  **Gulf Coast**

From what is known, using historical sources and archaeological data, the area known to scholars as *Mesoamerica* ("Middle America"), had a highly developed culture. In the 1500s, its territory was bounded on the north by the Panuco, Lerma, and Sinaloa rivers, and on the south by the Ulua River and the Gulf of Nicoya. Today the territory is divided by archaeologists into various regions or provinces, such as the Central Plateau, the Gulf Coast, Oaxaca, Maya, and Western Mexico.

### Early Evidence

In the excavations at Tlapacoya, Mexico, the fossil remains of mastodons, and other animals of the Pleistocene epoch were discovered. These findings were associated with tools such as scrapers, razors, and clubs. A fossilized human skull was also found. These remains are among the most recent finds in the Mexican Basin.

From the Teopisca Valley region (Chiapas), tools similar to those of the European Paleolithic period have been found. These included hand-held axes, scrapers, and strikers. From a gully at Caulapan (Puebla), comes a scraper dating from around 19,000 B.C. From the Chimalacatlan region (Morelos), come tools and the fossil remains of animals. Traces of ashes, coal, and flint proved that these people knew about fire. The remains of animal bones and plants in several caves are evidence that they used rock shelters and knew how to make basic tools.

### Nomadic Hunters

Between 20,000 and 12,000 B.C., people were gatherers of animal and plant foods. Shortly thereafter they began to use weapons. They used the *atlatl* (or spear thrower) as a weapon in hunting mammoth, bison, giant sloth, horse, and other Pleistocene animals. At Santa Isabel Ixtapan, for example, the remains of two mammoths were found. One had traces that showed that it was killed by a spear. The second bore signs of wounds by several weapons, as well as other tools. Hunters ranged over wide areas. They supplemented their diets with food-gathering. They lived in the open in rudimentary tents in encampments, but they also used caves. They wore animal skins for clothing, and they were acquainted with fire and more advanced stoneworking techniques. Several bone and tusk bead finds indicate that they wore ornaments.

### Gatherers Gain Knowledge

Climatic changes that occurred between 7000 and 5000 B.C. brought about the extinction of prehistoric fauna. People were forced to depend on woodland plants and small game. They ate mostly plant food, and remained in one area all year. They learned how to cultivate certain plants. By the end of this stage, people had learned to cultivate maize, beans, and peppers. The same period saw the use of the first millstones. The people made baskets, ropes, coarse cloth, sandals, and mats. The dead were buried in caves and sprinkled with cinnabar or powdered red hematite.

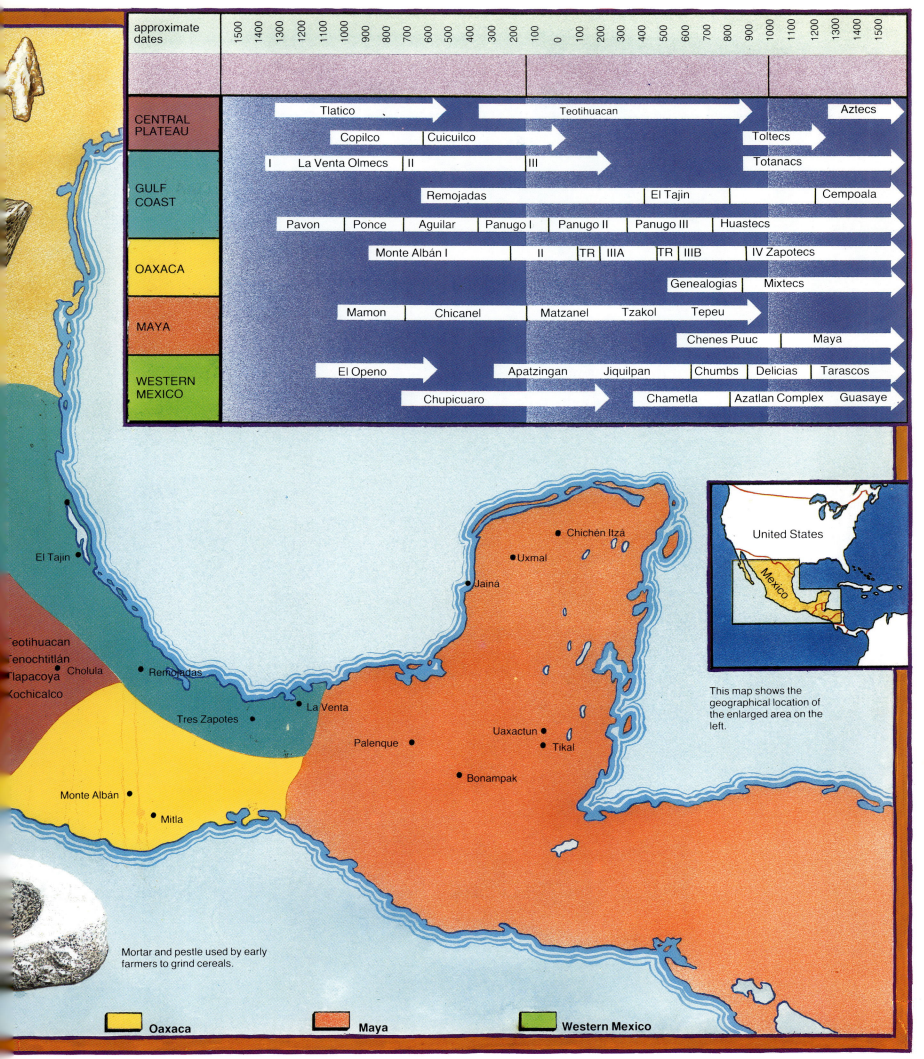

A vessel in the shape of a fish, found at Tlatilco.

A statuette representing a magician or shaman with a mask, found at Tlatilco.

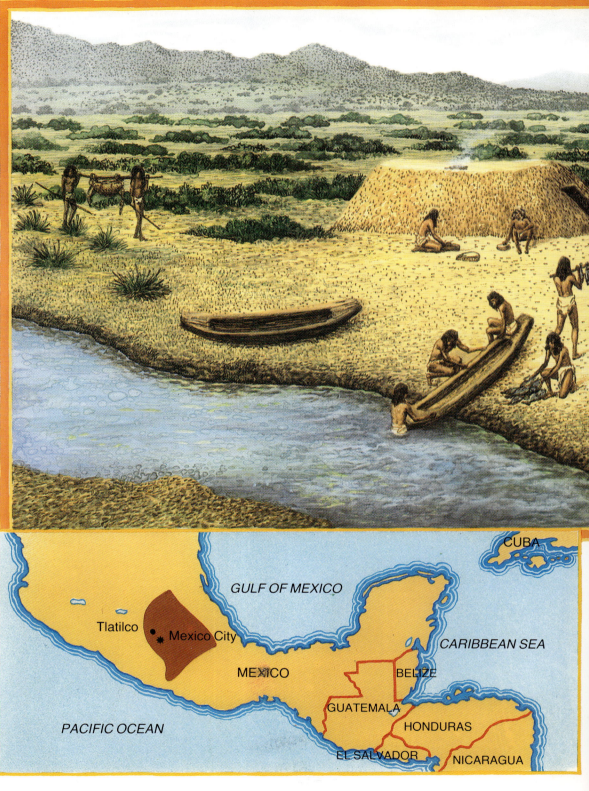

A map of the Mesoamerican region. The Central Plateau of Mexico is shown in red.

# THE CENTRAL PLATEAU OF MEXICO

## Village Life

Village life in the Mexican Basin goes back to the time of the first farmers about 5000 B.C. These people supplemented their diets by hunting, fishing, and food-gathering. As a result of the systematic cultivating of maize and of vegetable gathering, permanent dwellings began to be built in areas with dense populations.

When population increased, groups usually settled in places that had an abundant water supply. They built villages of huts made from a mixture of clay and straw. A noteworthy example is the locality known as Tlatilco (Mexico state). It was there that groups of farmers built huts on the sandy banks of the river. They took advantage of the periodic flooding to cultivate low-lying areas and to engage in fishing and various other activities.

These riverside dwellers were experts in making pottery. Its decoration reflects the life

A prehistoric village of Mexico's Central Plateau is reconstructed here. Notice that agricultural activity exists alongside other activities such as fishing and armadillo hunting. Pottery is made in an open hearth-pit. Houses consist of wooden supporting structures topped with coverings of earth and plant matter.

of the rivers and forests. Their works depict fish, ducks, tortoises, armadillos, wild boars, iguanas, hares, snakes, and coots. All of these species would have been abundant in the area.

Farmers tilled the soil with simple digging sticks. They probably stored their grain in the open. They fished, using canoes made of hollowed-out trees and nets. They also hunted, using light spears. Land was held in common, and every natural resource was put to use.

Further light has been shed on this culture by the hundreds of items found at grave sites. For example, bone needles and awls provide evidence of a weaving industry. Obsidian razors, knives, and scrapers imply cutting operations, such as butchering animals and preparing hides. Greenstone axes suggest carpentry.

In addition to these activities, the village had skilled potters, hatmakers, matmakers, fishers, hunters, and farmers. Authority was exercised by a group of headmen.

Figurines representing sorcerers or shamans wearing wigs and fearsome masks indicate these witch-priests held considerable power. Masks were much worn. Clay masks have been found modelled after jaguars, ducks, imaginary birds, and human beings.

Clothing consisted of a kind of trousers for men and short skirts for women. People of high rank wore tunics made of animal skin, headdresses, and sandals. They painted their hair, bodies, and faces, and arranged their braided hair around their faces. They wore earrings, necklaces, and bracelets of clay, bone, and seashells.

People of that time lived in a world of magic and spirits. The shaman acted as a medium between people and spirits. People and dogs were sacrificed at funerals of important people, in the belief that the sacrifices would accompany the dead people to the next world. The dead were buried in earthen pits with objects to be used in the other world. These objects included various types of crockery (occasionally with food inside), axes, stones for grinding grain, needles, spear points and arrowheads, whistles, necklaces of clay bells, and jewels. At Tlatilco it was believed that the spirit of water on earth was a water snake. The Olmecs introduced the image of the jaguar as a symbol of the earth. The two beasts eventually fused into one half-snake, half-cat monster, representing the earth made fertile by water.

31

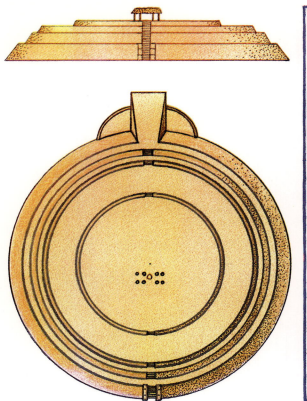 

Two views (*above*) plus a reconstruction (*above right*) show the temple of Cuicuilco with its monumental base. The shrine on top was built of perishable materials such as wood and plants. Circular in form, it is the oldest pyramidal construction to be discovered on the Mexican plateau. Cuicuilco was destroyed by the eruption of the volcano Xitle.
*Inset:* A brass object representing the god of fire (Huehuetotl) was found at Cuicuilco.

# RELIGIOUS CENTRES OF THE CENTRAL PLATEAU

## Cuicuilco

Several factors were responsible for the transformation of certain important villages into small religious centres. These factors included an increase in population, the arrival of people from the countryside, and widening kinship ties.

Cuicuilco is in the hills of the Central Plateau and Mexican Basin. It began as an ordinary agricultural village. With time it became a gathering place for people from nearby villages. Later Cuicuilco became a religious centre. It was the site of the first circular pyramid. From the outside, the pyramid looked like four discs piled on top of one another. Each disc was smaller than the one beneath it. Inside the pyramid were chambers with different religious uses. These included altars, one or more temples, a ritual chamber, tombs, and various other rooms.

## Pyramid Building

With the rise of religious centres, step-pyramids began to appear throughout the region. To cope with the increased construction, new tools were developed. These included chisels, plumb lines, levels, rollers, ropes, simple measuring instruments, and a cement mixture composed of lime and sand.

At the site of Tlapacoya, archaeologists found a step-pyramid that had been constructed in two stages. First, a wide platform with a central stairway was built around a hill. A structure of five inclined sections was then added. At the top was a *bajareque* temple (made of clay, straw, and palm fronds). During this second stage, three tombs with stone walls were added in the centre of the building. This development of Mexican Basin religious centres occurred between 800 and 200 B.C.

*Right:* the temple of Tlapacoya.

# THE TEOTIHUACAN

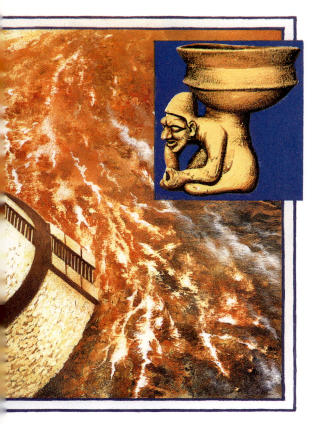

## A Valley for the Future "City of the Gods"

In the year 500 B.C., the Teotihuacan Valley of Mexico was occupied by groups of farmers. Many of the people in this area had moved from the western basin after a volcano eruption. These people established villages on mountain spurs and slopes and in flat areas. It was in this way that such centres as Maquizco, Patlachique, and Cuanalan came into being. As time passed, some of these people settled in the central region of the valley. They began constructing platforms, enclosed dwellings, and step-pyramids that were made of stone cemented with clay.

About 100 B.C., work began on the so-called Pyramid of the Sun. This gigantic step-pyramid is about 66 metres high. It consists of five inclined sections, which are filled with earth and covered with plaster. Some time later, work began on the so-called Pyramid of the Moon. It was similar to the Pyramid of the Sun, but it was filled with stones. Construction of the two pyramids went on until A.D 100.

Along the axis of the two pyramids there was a wide avenue called the Street of the Dead. It was 5 kilometres long. Buildings were gradually erected on both sides of the street. The Teotihuacan builders laid out a series of temples, built to the same basic plan of inclined and horizontal sections. Examples include the Temple of Agriculture, the Temple of Mythological Animals and the so-called Temple of Quetzalcóatl (A.D. 100-350).

The Temple of Quetzalcóatl (the Plumed Serpent) is decorated with mosaic, using plaster and painted stones. The theme on the *talud* (inclined plane) is a plumed serpent coupled with motifs of snails, starfish, and seashells. On the *tablero* (cornice), a plumed serpent alternates with a being with a scaled body. The *tablero* serpent could be a raincloud in the form of a celestial dragon. The scaly monster might stand for fire, a light beam, or lightning. The *talud* serpents, on the other hand, probably symbolize the waters of the earth which have fallen from the sky to fill the rivers and lakes.

## A Great Metropolis

The period between A.D. 350 and 750 was the golden age of Teotihuacan as a great religious, political, and administrative centre. Workers completed the buildings along the Street of the Dead, the Plaza of the Moon, the Temple of the Plumed Snails, and the Citadel. Numerous buildings were constructed with many rooms, a single entrance, and several stairways. These buildings were organized into districts with many palaces and temples. During this stage, the city grew to about 18 square kilometres in area.

## Murals and Gods

At Teotihuacan, the painting of murals grew into a highly developed art. Interior walls and occasionally even exterior walls were prepared with plaster. The figures and scenes were first sketched and then each was differentiated and defined. Finally, they were outlined and enclosed with a dark shade of amaranth. The best-known murals are those of El Paraiso de Tlaloc (Tlalocan), the Temples of the Mythological Animals and Agriculture, the decorations at the Palace of Atetelco, and the Temple of the Eaglets or Quetzal.

Since Teotihuacan was also a religious capital, festivals were celebrated in the great plazas in honour of various divinities. Among these divinities were the Serpent Rain Cloud; Huehueteotl, the old god of fire; Tlaloc, the god of rain and harvests; Chalchiuhtlicue, the goddess of earthly waters and food; Xipe, the god of spring; and Quetzalcóatl, the Plumed Serpent.

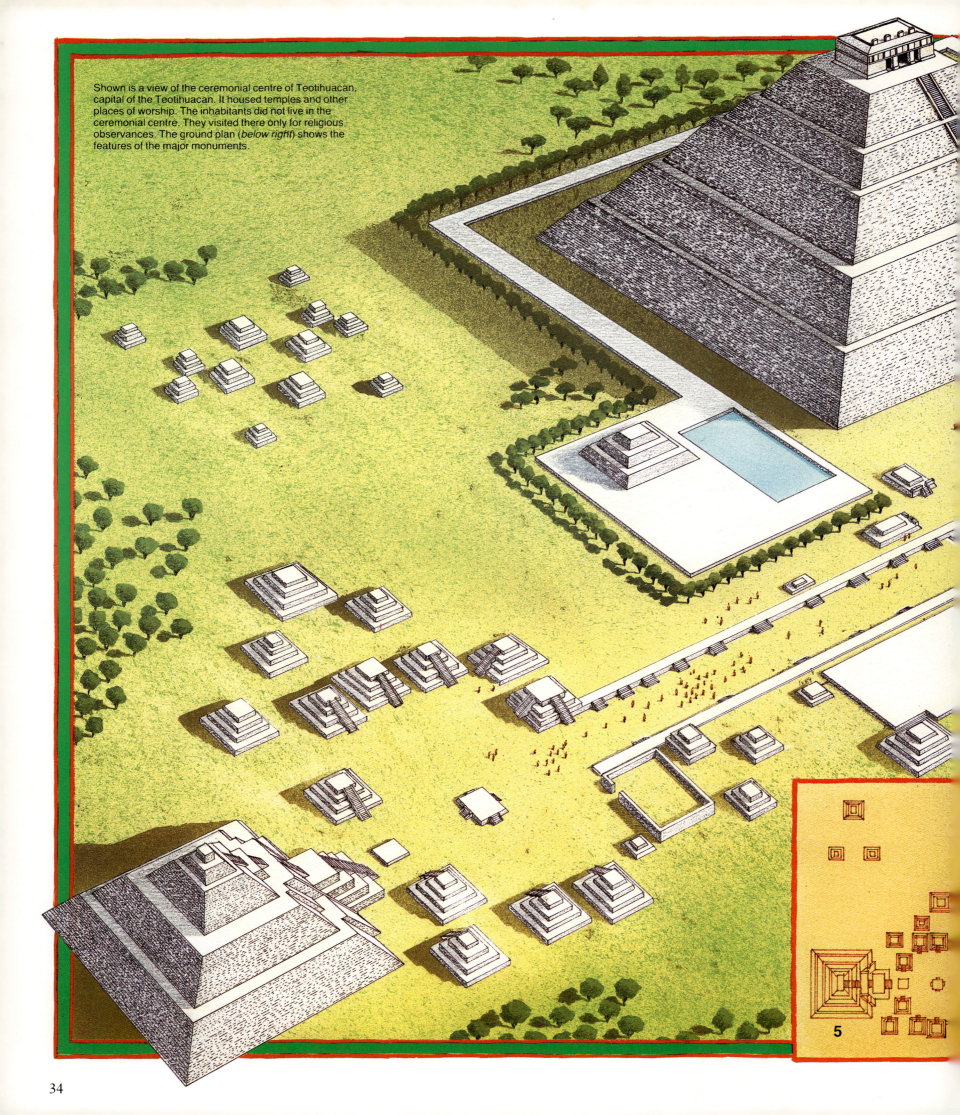

Shown is a view of the ceremonial centre of Teotihuacan, capital of the Teotihuacan. It housed temples and other places of worship. The inhabitants did not live in the ceremonial centre. They visited there only for religious observances. The ground plan (*below right*) shows the features of the major monuments.

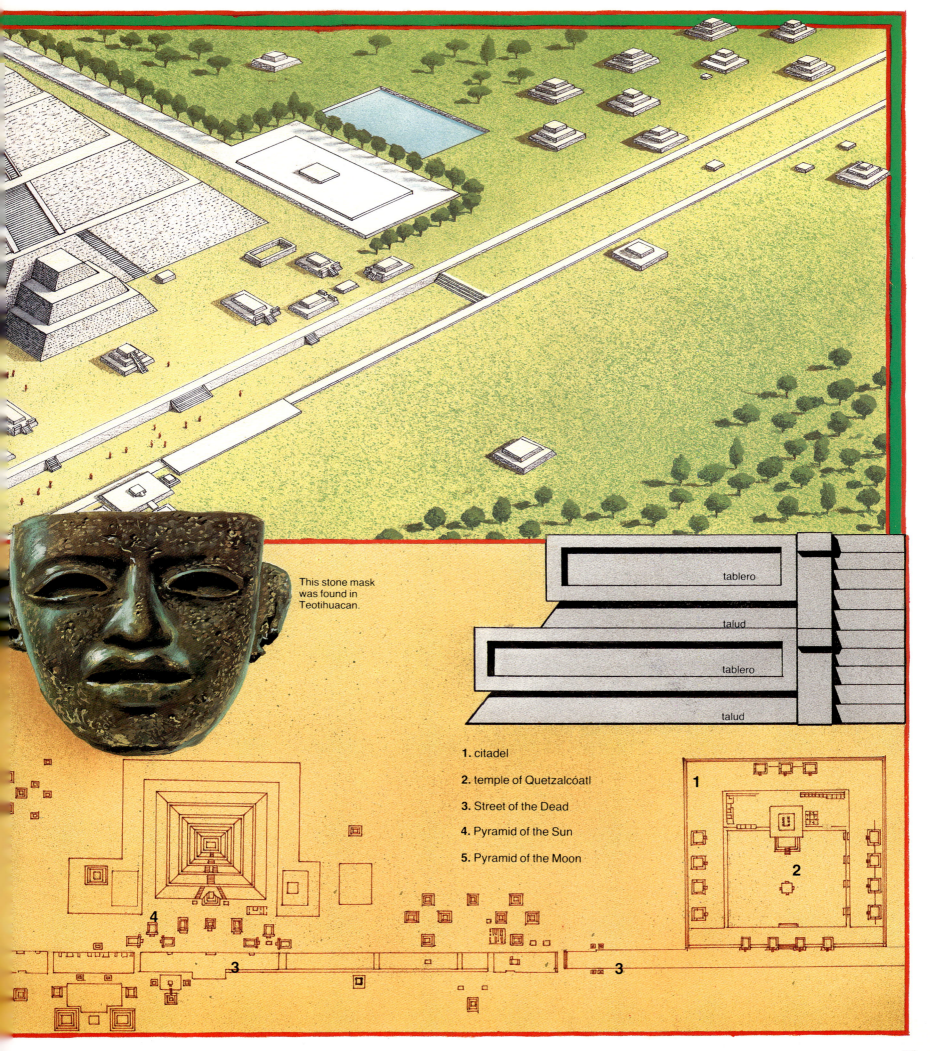

This stone mask was found in Teotihuacan.

tablero
talud
tablero
talud

1. citadel
2. temple of Quetzalcóatl
3. Street of the Dead
4. Pyramid of the Sun
5. Pyramid of the Moon

# THE TOLTECS

## A Mysterious People

After the fall of Teotihuacan, many people left the Mexican Basin in search of new land. This was the case with the Toltecs, a mysterious people who ruled an empire from a capital called Tollan.

According to the codex, or history, called the *Annals of Cuauhitlan*, a warrior named Mixcoatl had a son by a woman named Chimalma. The baby was named Ce Acatl Topiltzin (Lord One Cane) with the added title of Quetzalcóatl, the divinity he was supposed to personify.

Acatl grew up in the region of Morelos. When he became an adult, he moved to the lands of Guanajuato and Huasteca. There, the Toltecs rejoined him in order to create the foundations for a kingdom in the city of Tollan, present-day Tula in Mexico.

The Toltecs brought together groups of Otoms, Teotihuacans, and Chichimecs. They founded their city at a site between El Corral and the area to the west. Very little is known about the early period of the city's history. More information exists, however, about the period of the highest success of the cult of Quetzalcóatl, under the Mayan influence.

## Tula's Peak of Development

During this stage, an enormous plaza with an altar in the centre was built. It was reached by a stairway that had decorated friezes on the sides.

On one side of the plaza, a great step-pyramid was erected. Nearby, a rectangular structure was constructed adjacent to the major buildings. The most important building was the Temple of Tlahuizcalpantecuhtli. Designs on the structure included motifs of processions of jaguars and coyotes moving in opposite directions, eagles tearing at human hearts, and effigies of the Man-Bird-Serpent, the god Quetzalcóatl.

Not much remains of Tula. The bottom insert shows the present-day ruins of the great ceremonial platform and an imagined reconstruction of the upper-level shrine. The spectacular columns give a hint of the monument's former grandeur.

On the upper part there was a temple. Its facade had two columns in the form of serpents, their heads on the bottom and their tails on top. The rest of the temple rested on four rows of columns decorated with images that included warriors, nobles, and earth symbols.

An imposing wall stood behind this building. It was decorated with halved seashells (symbols of the wind), and it had a large frieze in bas-relief. The main motif of the edges has a serpent swallowing a skeleton-like figure.

After the Temple of Tlahuizcalpantecuhtli, the Burnt Palace was built. It had a portico of columns covered with four stone slabs. Inside were altars with *chacmol* decoration and a frieze. The *chacmol* are warriors with containers on their stomachs in wait for the human hearts about to be sacrificed. The frieze depicts a winding procession of warriors and priests in parade dress.

## Warriors and Skilled Artisans

Certain facts became apparent from these discoveries. It is obvious that the god Quetzalcóatl was worshipped at Tula, and that the population included skilled artisans. These included whitewashers, painters, masons, carpenters, plasterers, stonecutters, and featherworkers. It is also known that during that period there developed the style of the serpentine columns, the *chacmol*, the bench-lined walls, the columns decorated with images of warriors, and the porticos and colonnades of the type found at various sites in Yucatán.

The dates A.D. 900 and 1168 mark the beginning and end of the history of Tula. During this period, the city prevailed over other less-advanced peoples and formed alliances. Little evidence of the Toltec city remains. But its level of civilization placed it chiefly in a position of undisputed power over the other cultures of Mexico.

# THE AZTECS

The Aztecs originated as nomadic tribes from northern Mesoamerica. They moved to the Mexican Basin, together with other groups who, like themselves, were searching for land. After passing through various areas, including the area around Tula, they reached the Chapultepec region.

Since most of the land was already occupied, the Aztecs were almost constantly at war. To avoid conflict, they moved to a small island and there founded their capital, Tenochtitlán, in 1325.

With great effort, they brought materials from the mainland and began the construction of a great metropolis. The city stood as a great cultural, political, and administrative centre. It was defended by four walls, which had four gates decorated with serpents. From each gate a road led from the island to the mainland.

The Aztecs constructed dams, barriers, and aqueducts to keep the salt water out of the city's water supply. They built public fountains, streets made of logs and pounded earth, and created a vast system of canals. In the centre of the city was the Major Temple, a symbol of power. It had two stairways with friezes ending in cubic motifs. The stairs led to two identical temples. One honoured the god of rain, the other the god of war.

Facing the Major Temple was another cone-shaped temple in honour of the god of the wind. Other temples were dedicated to numerous gods. There were also military depots, warehouses, halls for poets and singers, and libraries. Close to the centre of the city were the palaces of the governors of Axayacatl and Montezuma.

## A Cosmopolitan Centre

The economy of the Aztecs was based on agriculture and goods made by artisans. The products were usually sold in markets. Economic demand for the products was high, and merchants sold their goods in surrounding areas. These areas extended along the coast as far as Xicalango and also through Puebla and Oaxaca and on into Soconusco.

The greatest demand was for high-quality and exotic goods. These included jade, rock crystals, jewels, bracelets of precious metals, objects made from tortoise shells, plumes from the quetzal bird, and jaguar skins.

In Tenochtitlán worked artisans of all sorts, including jewellers, featherworkers, stone-cutters, and artists. There were also sculptors, architects, experts in hydraulics, doctors, writers, and poets. Many artisans from other regions came to Tenochtitlán, attracted by the city's power and splendour.

The warrior class had the most power in the city. Next to them were the priests. Their main task was to spread their religion to conquered people. The priests also organized celebrations to honour the gods.

The union of the gods Ometecuhtli and Oecihuatl produced four offspring, called the Tezcatlipocas. One of these deities was Quetzalcóatl and another Huitzilopochtli. Other Aztec divinities were Huehueteotl, lord of fire; Tlaloc, lord of rain; and Xipe Totec, patron of the spring and the produce of the earth.

Map showing Tenochtitlán and the numerous small regional centres dependent on the capital. This region corresponds to the small rectangle shown on the map at right.

In the heart of Tenochtitlán, there arose the ceremonial centre, a vast four-sided structure measuring 300 metres along each side. Its double walls enclosed temples and other ritual buildings, in addition to the emperor's quarters. It was made of square rock blocks and lime, either white or painted in bright colours. The centre was dominated by the major temple (1) which stood about 60 metres high. A series of 114 steps lead up to two small twin-pyramids with statues of Huitzilopochtli, god of war, and Tlaloc, god of rain, adorned with gold and precious stones, whom the Aztecs honoured with human sacrifices. The circular temple of the god of the wind rose in front of the major centre (2). A little farther on, there rose the site where ball games were played (3), and on the right, was the temple of Tezcatlipoca, god of darkness (4). The priests lived in a building with a terraced roof (5). To the south, extended the great palace of Montezuma (6). This reproduction is based on a model in the Museum of Anthropology in Mexico City.

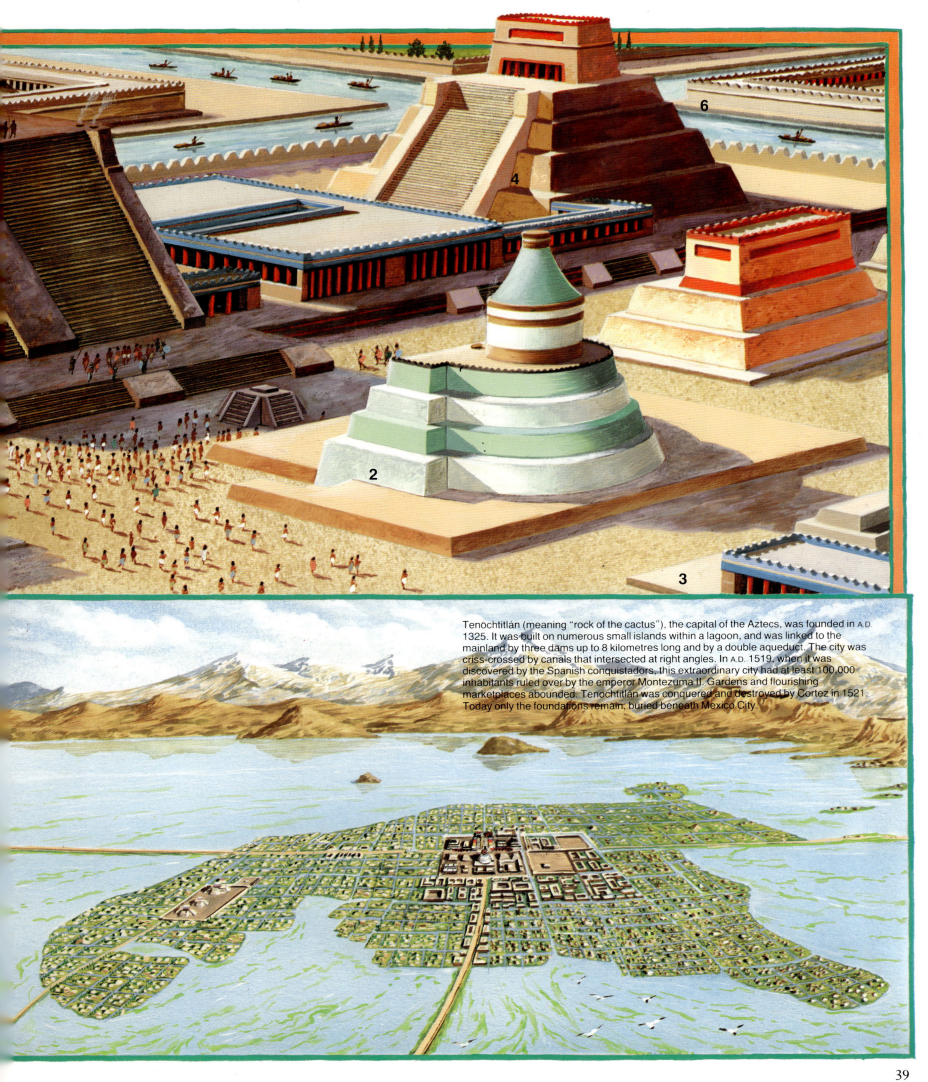

Tenochtitlán (meaning "rock of the cactus"), the capital of the Aztecs, was founded in A.D. 1325. It was built on numerous small islands within a lagoon, and was linked to the mainland by three dams up to 8 kilometres long and by a double aqueduct. The city was criss-crossed by canals that intersected at right angles. In A.D. 1519, when it was discovered by the Spanish conquistadors, this extraordinary city had at least 100,000 inhabitants ruled over by the emperor Montezuma II. Gardens and flourishing marketplaces abounded. Tenochtitlán was conquered and destroyed by Cortez in 1521. Today only the foundations remain, buried beneath Mexico City.

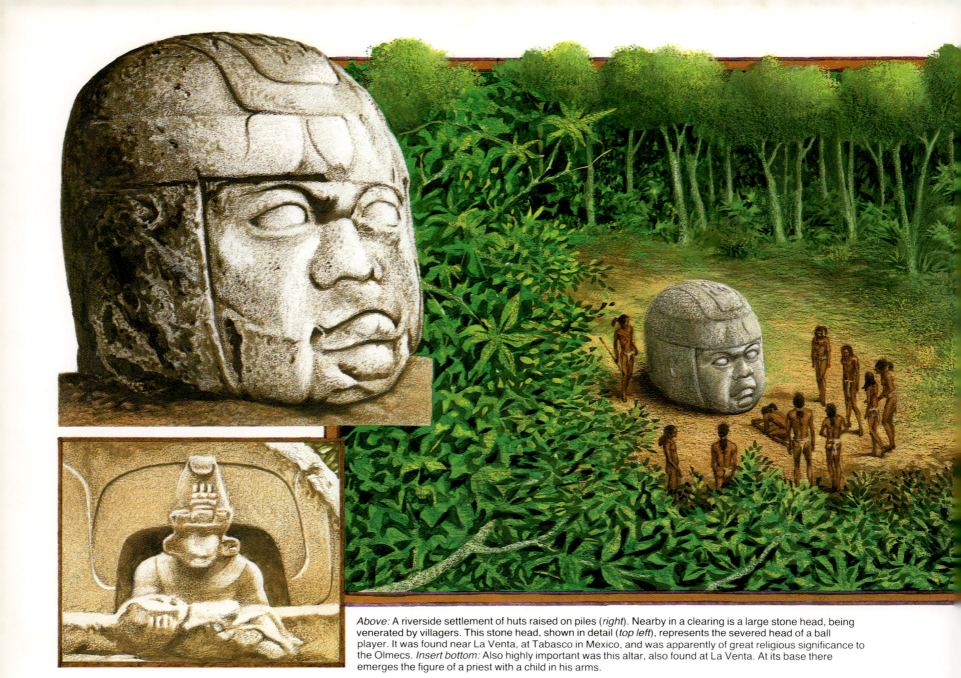

*Above:* A riverside settlement of huts raised on piles (*right*). Nearby in a clearing is a large stone head, being venerated by villagers. This stone head, shown in detail (*top left*), represents the severed head of a ball player. It was found near La Venta, at Tabasco in Mexico, and was apparently of great religious significance to the Olmecs. *Insert bottom:* Also highly important was this altar, also found at La Venta. At its base there emerges the figure of a priest with a child in his arms.

# THE OLMECS

## The Land of Rubber

Mysterious artistic people once lived in Los Tuxtlas, the forest south of Vera Cruz, and in the marshes of Tabasco. These groups were called Olmecs. They were from Olman, literally "the land of rubber". Some scholars believe that the Olmecs arrived in migrant waves from as far south as Ecuador. Some of them made their way as far as Oaxaca, Guerrero, Puebla, Morelos, and the Mexican Basin. Others crossed the Isthmus of Tehuantepec and reached the Gulf Coast. Wherever they went, they left a distinct culture.

Around 2400 B.C., Olmec influence led to a tradition of coarse, plain pottery. But around 1700 B.C., there was a tradition rich in decorative motifs: impressions made with cords and fabric, with fingernails, and with combs, for example. These motifs had already been used in Ecuador, Colombia, and other places from about 3000 and 2500 B.C.

The Olmecs introduced other innovations. These included travel by means of rafts and canoes, the construction of pile-dwellings and palisades, and the planting of tubers such as the yucca.

## Olmec Villages

From 1700 to 1200 B.C., there was an Olmec village stage marked by the penetration, spreading, and stabilization of Olmec culture within lands that were occupied by other peoples or within lands that were unpopulated. This occurred from Altamira (Chiapas) to Tlatilco in the Mexican Basin, and from Oaxaca to the Gulf Coast.

At Tres Zapotes and San Lorenzo (Vera Cruz) and at La Venta (Tabasco), archaeologists have found pottery with decorations of the claws, spots, teeth, and eyelashes of the

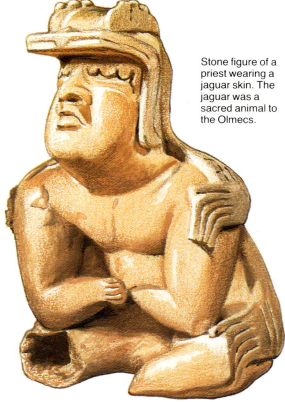

Stone figure of a priest wearing a jaguar skin. The jaguar was a sacred animal to the Olmecs.

On this map, the spread of Olmec art objects is indicated in red.

jaguar. The jaguar was both feared and venerated, and symbolized earth and fertility. Also popular was a type of pottery that was black with a white rim or white with a black rim.

The Olmecs preferred to settle near waterways and forests. During this village stage, the organization of clans flourished, and trade with the Central Plateau prospered.

## Religious Centres

The Olmec civilization lasted from about 1200 to 100 B.C. The height of their power coincided with rule by a theocracy which initiated the construction of earthen mounds and temples made of clay and straw. Religious centres were built, with living quarters, residences for distinguished people, and other structures. Earth was the only building material used. These religious centres were identified by sculptures, including huge stone heads. Some of the heads were more than 2 metres high.

The heads are probably likenesses of victims offered in sacrifice on the occasion of pelota games. The stone heads subsequently served as a protective totem for the community.

## The Olmec Culture

Other noteworthy sculptures included great stone containers resembling coffins, sculptures of priests wearing jaguar masks, and floor mosaics of green stones with jaguar heads. The Olmecs made axes carved in the form of flower petals, masks, earrings, and necklaces.

The Olmecs also produced statues and headstones, inscribed with hieroglyphics and circles with numerical values. Some experts believe that the Olmecs developed a calendar and a number system. The Olmec expansion affected all of Mesoamerica.

# THE ZAPOTECS

The Zapotec Indians settled in the mountain valleys and along the coast of what is now the Mexican state of Oaxaca. The ruins of their settlements can still be seen.

## Monte Albán

The Zapotecs built a temple complex called Monte Albán, levelling the top of a mountain to create the site. Monte Albán was constructed in stages between A.D. 1 and 900. During the first stage, the Temple of the Dancers was built. It had high walls, which were covered with huge stone slabs. Human figures were depicted on the walls.

A major structure from the second stage is five-sided and shaped like an arrowhead. One section was possibly used as an astronomical observatory. During the same stage an arena for playing ball games was built.

## Tombs

The Zapotecs produced a lot of funerary architecture. The first tombs were long, horizontal structures that had stone walls and were covered with stone slabs. They were buried under houses or courtyards. Later tombs had vertical walls, vaulted covers, and roofs with eaves made of stone slabs. Finally, tombs were built with flights of steps and a facade with a niche in the centre to hold the statue of a god. An antechamber and a burial chamber were later added with niches in the bottom and side walls. Some tombs had murals on their interior walls. Usually, several bodies were placed in one large sarcophagus. Only important people had individual tombs. Clay urns placed in the sarcophagus were for use in the afterlife.

## Hieroglyphics, Numbers, and Pottery

Numbers, writing, and the calendar all came into use in the Zapotec culture. Numbers were expressed using symbols of hands and fingers or dots and bars. Hieroglyphics or picture-signs were used in ornamental scrolls. There were signs for the sun, an emerald, a jaguar head, a boot, a bat, a hill, and so forth. Later on, inscriptions and stories were carved on monuments and stone slabs. Monte Albán pottery was grey and black only, but displays originality and variety.

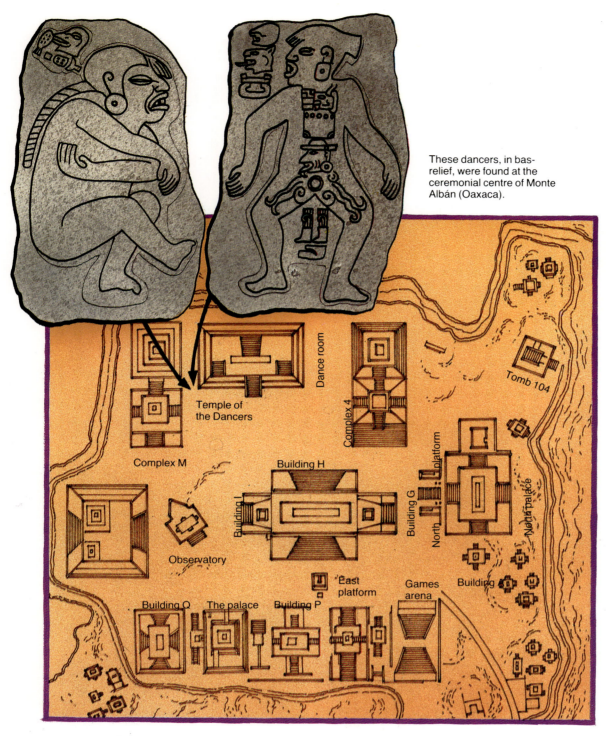

These dancers, in bas-relief, were found at the ceremonial centre of Monte Albán (Oaxaca).

Above: Plan of Monte Albán. The various structures are identified by numbers, names, and letters. The dwellings of important persons were probably located on the eastern platform and in the palaces. Many of the other buildings were probably used for ceremonial purposes.

Left: The ruins of Monte Albán. The mountain-top site commanded the surrounding countryside.

# THE MIXTECS

Existing at the same time as Monte Albán were the other cultures, whose remains have been found at San Jose Mogote and Dainzu. Remains of a platform with a casing of huge stone blocks were found at Dainzu. On the blocks were pictures of ball players.

The Zapotecs lived in Montenegro, Cuilapan, Quiotepec, Lambitieco, Yagul, and other cities. But toward the end of the Monte Albán period, they were no longer the dominant group. The Mixtecs now began to govern the Zapotecs. Evidence of this is provided by a Monte Albán tomb that had been built by the Zapotecs but reused for the burial of a Mixtec lord.

Oaxaca is a mountainous region, and it was chosen for this reason by the Mixtecs, who were called "people of the clouds and the mists". It is not clear exactly where they came from, but it is likely that they first settled in the region of Terra Caliente, between Guerrero and Canada del Tomellin (in Puebla state, Mexico). They later moved into the surrounding mountains.

According to some records, the Mixtecs were already present in the mountains around A.D. 700. They began to form small territories. After having appropriated neighbouring lands in the valley, they later reached Mitla and Monte Albán.

The Mixtecs were a warlike people. They were also highly skilled at crafts. Craftspeople used a mosaic technique which employed plastered and painted stones. At Mitla, this style reached its pinnacle; it was accompanied by masterly threshold designs and stone columns. Occasionally, motifs of key-patterns and red figures were painted on the lintels.

## Goldsmiths and Stone-Carvers

The Mixtecs usually buried their leaders in cross-shaped tombs or in tombs with an antechamber, a burial chamber, and niches. The bodies of sacrificial victims were put in the antechamber to serve as companions and servants to the dead leader in the afterlife. The lord's body was placed in the inner chamber, together with a collection of funerary offerings and one additional slave-victim whose task it was to provide for the deceased's immediate needs.

In tombs at both Monte Albán and Zaachila, the remains have been found of the bodies of Mixtec lords with rich funerary offerings of rings, earrings, and gold breastplates and necklaces. Mosaics of seashells and turquoise stones, small vases, beads of rock crystal and jade, and other treasures were also found. The Mixtecs were skilful metalworkers and goldsmiths. They made alloys; for example, a type of brass (a mixture of zinc and copper). They were also adept at various techniques such as hammering, laminating, soldering, and filigree work. The Mixtecs were skilful carvers of rock crystal, bone, and wood. They also created subtle mosaics composed of turquoise stones, seashells, jade, and other materials.

The Mixtecs were excellent potters. They made a wide variety of multi-coloured, glazed pottery. Three-legged vessels in the shape of animals, basins, cups, and objects in the form of various beasts have been found. All were decorated with motifs such as key-patterns and flowers. The colours used included amaranth red, yellow, white, black, and grey.

## Evidence from the Codices

The *codices* were "books" in picture-writing. They were long strips of tanned animal hides arranged in accordion folds. On them were narrative accounts of genealogies, marriages, natural surroundings, military conquests, deities, and festivals. Among the most notable are the Borgia, Vindobonensis, and Bodley-Selden codices. The codices tell the story of a Zapotec princess married to a Mixtec lord. Decorations on a Mixtec house also document an alliance between the two groups.

The Mixtec provinces often fought one another to seize fresh territory. They were, however, united into a confederation against the Aztecs. This was the situation before the arrival of the Spaniards.

Cojico, god of rain, was the principal Zapotec deity. Cojico's image has been found on many funeral urns.

Refined architecture was characteristic of the palace at Mitla (Oaxaca), the city founded by the Mixtecs.

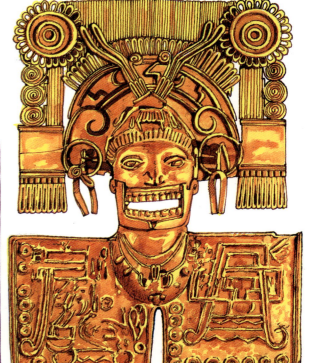

A gold breast-plate depicts the god of death. Mixtec goldsmiths have been credited with this work which was found in a Monte Albán tomb.

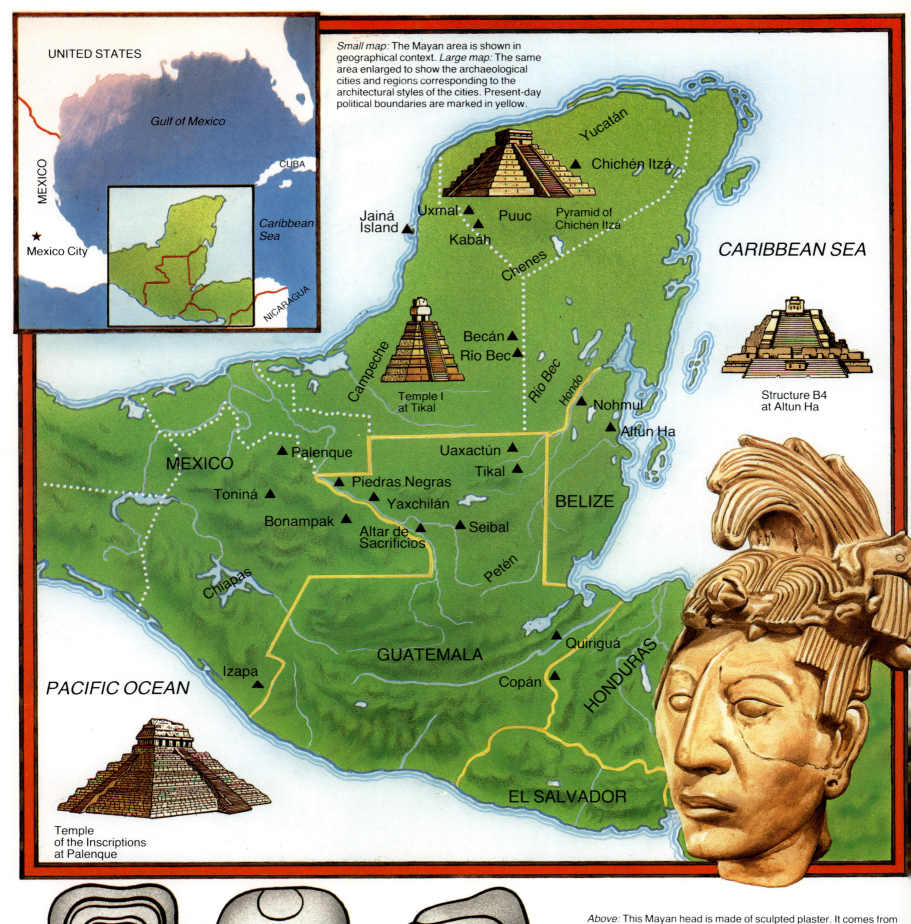

*Small map:* The Mayan area is shown in geographical context. *Large map:* The same area enlarged to show the archaeological cities and regions corresponding to the architectural styles of the cities. Present-day political boundaries are marked in yellow.

Structure B4 at Altun Ha

Temple I at Tikal

Pyramid of Chichén Itzá

Temple of the Inscriptions at Palenque

*Above:* This Mayan head is made of sculpted plaster. It comes from the chamber of the Temple of the Inscriptions, Palenque.

*Left:* Each Mayan city had an emblem, perhaps hieroglyphics, indicating its name. From left to right are the emblems of Tikal, Palenque, and Yaxchilán.

# THE MAYA

The Maya were probably once a group of people that lived by hunting and gathering. At some point, Maya villages in Guatemala had an unusual rate of expansion. Groups began to move toward the Yucatán. Numerous villages arose along the Hondo River between 2500 and 1000 B.C.

From that time, a proliferation of villages took place throughout the Mayan area. Religious centres later grew up near these villages. These centres include Tikal, Uaxactun, Holmul, Mountain Cow, Balakbal, Becan, Rio Bec, Oxkintok, and Dzibilchaltun. They appeared between 500 and 400 B.C.

During that period, along the Pacific Coast from Chiapas (Mexico) to Guatemala, the Izapa style of sculpture spread. Its main expression was in bas-reliefs with scenes of a religious and mythic nature. Occasionally, scenes showed daily life. This style left its traces in the interior region of Guatemala, where the first monuments and inscriptions appeared. The first typically Mayan monument is that of Tikal (A.D. 250-300).

## Astronomers, Mathematicians, and Scribes

The Maya were a people of short stature with straight hair, slanted eyes, protruding cheekbones, and aquiline noses. They used somewhat drastic cosmetic techniques, such as altering the skull, cutting teeth, and embedding precious stones in the flesh.

The Maya were expert astronomers and mathematicians. They introduced the use of zero and invented a number system which progressed by multiples of 20—that is to say, 20, 400, 8000, 160,000 and so on. A system of dots and bars was used to write numbers. They used a religious calendar of 260 days, which they called a Tzolkin. They also used a solar calendar of 365 days, which they called a Haab. There were 20 days to a month, 18 months to a year, with 5 days left over.

They were skilled artisans. The scribes documented important events of the time first on stone and then in the codices. Unfortunately, there are only three surviving codices.

At the time of the Spanish conquest (beginning in 1517), the Maya were already in marked decline. Their cities and minor centres were regrouped into provinces, or *caciquates*, such as Ecab, Sotuta, Mani Chikinchel, and Hocaba.

A Mayan lord receives the gift of a jaguar head in this bas-relief at Yaxchilán.

This representation of social stratification in the pre-Hispanic Mayan world was inspired by the murals at Bonampak. At the top of the pyramid is the lord Halachuinic meaning "true man". On the lower levels are nobles, warriors, artisans and merchants, and at the bottom peasants.

This sculpture depicts a priestess in front of a temple. It comes from the Island of Jainá, a location known for its pottery.

# A MAYAN CITY—CHICHÉN ITZÁ

Mayan cities in different regions display distinct differences in style. The Peten style was characterized by enormous platforms to which other structures were attached. The great step-pyramids were topped by temples defended by battlements.

The Palenque style, on the other hand, consisted of low structures with smoothly surfaced bases and temples resembling stone huts. Each temple had a corridor and two rooms (portico and sanctuary) on the inside, battlements on the roof, and two external facades decorated with painted figures and motifs of moulded plaster.

The Rio Bec style was distinguished by ornamental towers positioned at the ends of elongated buildings. The base-temples had a central gate flanked by gigantic serpent masks. The Chenes style made use of similar elements, such as large frontal masks consisting of mosaics of plastered stone.

## The City of Wells

*Chichen Itzá* means "wells of the Itza". The name was given to the Mayan city after the Spanish conquest. The city is located in a hilly region of the Yucatán plateau, where there a

no rivers. Rainwater, however, filters into the limestone rock. This water-bearing layer is tapped through large natural wells called *cenotes*. Chichén Itzá was founded near two deep cenotes. Many finds were recovered from inside the wells.

The history of the city has become a topic of yet unresolved debate. An earlier settlement may have been invaded in the 900s either by the Toltecs or by the Maya from the Gulf Coast. A people known as the Itzá are mentioned as invaders both in its own narratives and in Spanish documents. Some scholars identify these people with the Toltecs, others with the Maya. There may have been a succession of occupations. In any case, it is evident that Chichén Itzá was a powerful centre. After the fall of the classical cities, Mayan civilization survived through the splendour of Chichén Itzá, which became a remarkable blend of numerous artistic styles.

Chichén Itzá, with (*below*) a plan of the buildings on the site. Important buildings were the so-called "castle", a nine-step pyramid with staircase and inner temple, the Temple of the Warriors, the Thousand Columns (where perhaps a marketplace was found), and the Nuns Temple (a complex of buildings which appears to have housed both residences and a temple). Nearby stand the two small temples, known as Colorado House and the Caracol, and the ball court. *Also below:* **1)** This sculpture of a half-reclining figure is of the Chac Mool, or divine messenger. It comes from the castle. On its stomach, it holds a plate with an offering to the sun. **2)** The eastern face of the Nuns Temple is decorated in Chenes style. **3)** A mosaic disc was found in the sacred well.

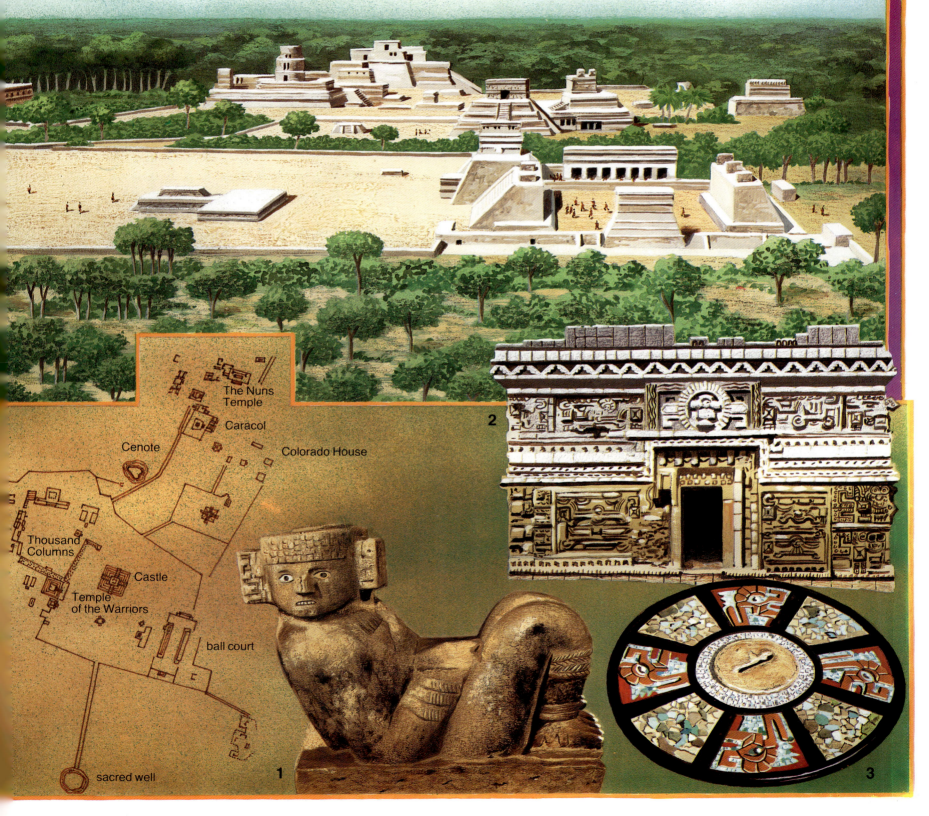

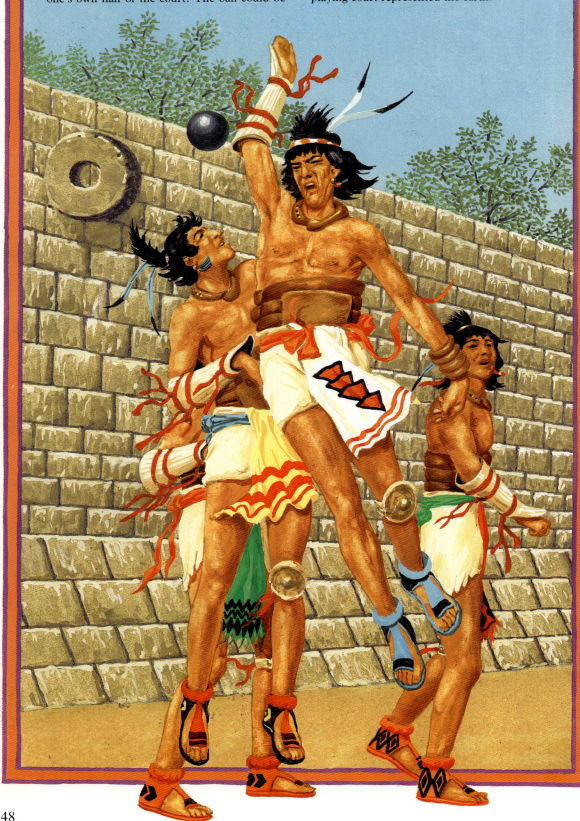

**The Ball Game**

The most widespread game in Mesoamerica was a ball game resembling pelota. It varied greatly in its rules, type of court, number of players, and size of ball. Many courts and detailed evidence are to be found in the Veracruz region. The game was played by two teams using a latex rubber ball, on a court with both flat and sloping side walls. Spanish chroniclers have told how the game (called *tlaxtli*) was played among the Aztecs. The object was to prevent the ball from entering one's own half of the court. The ball could be hit with the shoulders, forearms, elbows, and hips. The players strove to knock the ball through stone rings on the walls, in order to win the game.

The Maya called a similar game *pok-a-tok*, but not much is known about it. The playing arenas remain, usually in the shape of an "I," marked in the middle and on the sides by stone signals often found at temple sites. This game was both a sport and a religious rite. The ball's path symbolized the sun's orbit, and the playing court represented the earth.

# VERACRUZ

The Veracruz region of Mexico is on the east coast, facing the Gulf of Mexico. Various peoples who lived here are grouped together as the Veracruz Centre cultures. From at least 1500 B.C. onwards, such sites as El Trapiche, Chalahuite, and Viejon were active. They produced pottery that was richly decorated. These people were succeeded by the Remojadas complex, consisting of a number of farming villages. Their products included a red-coloured pottery.

The second stage of the Remojadas culture began with the construction of burial mounds. The body of the deceased was placed in the centre of the mound along with funerary offerings. The burial was then covered over with earth. These earthen mounds were later used as bases for temples and were eventually organized into complex structures.

## Sculpture

The third stage was the high point of the Veracruz Centre culture. Groups of people of unknown origin settled in places such as Xiuhtetelco, Quiahuiztlan, and El Tajin. Great cities arose. Architecture was marked by the use of the *talud* and *tablero* forms (see page 35), the latter surmounted by a cornice, using brick-sized slabs with receding and protruding motifs to form recesses. The recesses were then plastered and painted. The bases, consisting of superimposed sections, had a central stairway with friezes and recesses along the sides. Decorations included key-patterns and bas-reliefs and scenes showing the pelota game.

In the same period, builders produced columns formed of finely carved drum-shaped stones. The ball game inspired the making of stone "yokes", like the protective belts worn by the players, and "catcher's gloves". There are also a number of "smiling" clay figurines with large heads, and a broad, serene smile.

## New Migrations

These groups occupied Papantla, Misantla, and other localities in which they are still found. Driven on by invasions of Toltecs and Aztecs, other groups arrived and mingled with the earlier ones. One of these was the Totonac group which, after crossing the Zempoala plains, settled at Veracruz, Quiahuiztlan, and Boca Andrea.

Totonicapán was situated in the centre of the Veracruz region. Its territory was divided into three areas—the plains, the mountains, and the plateau. There were peaks up to 2,000 metres high. Groups of people settled along the rivers or in enclosed valleys. This region included the states of Hidalgo and San Luis Potosi, as well as the Huastesca area of Veracruz.

## The Totonacs

Practically speaking, Totonicapán is equivalent to the Gulf Coast of Mexico. The name means "where maize, the food, abounds". Between A.D. 900 and 1000, the Totonacs had already settled in this region and were beginning to expand.

Their style of architecture was similar to that of the Aztecs—two identical temples and a double-stairway with the frieze replaced by cubes. Other buildings had a line of battlements along the top. Plazas were wide.

Potters produced a refined orange-coloured pottery that was decorated with bas-reliefs and painted black. A multi-coloured pottery also existed. A number of enormous figures of gods, made of painted clay, have been found.

Totonicapán was responsible for several innovations in agriculture. These included the use of seedbeds for plant propagation and rearing. Irrigation canals were also used. When the Spaniards reached Zempoala, they were dazzled by the splendour of the dwellings. It was the first contact between the European invaders and the native cultures of Mesoamerica.

An impression of the sacred city of El Tajin (Veracruz). In the foreground is the structure known as the Pyramid of Niches.

*Right:* Stone reproductions of equipment used by ball players from the Veracruz region. These reproductions were intended for funeral use. On the bottom is a yoke or belt to protect the hips and act as a ball deflector. On the top right is a "glove" in the form of joined hands. This was probably used to catch and throw the ball. The other object probably represents the head of a player with a helmet in the shape of a dolphin.

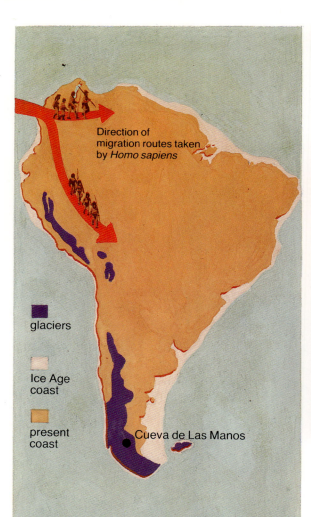

### South America in the Last Ice Age

In South America, glaciers reached their maximum extension by about 17,000 B.C. Large ice caps formed only in the extreme south. The continental glacier covered all the Tierra del Fuego region and the area of the Patagonian Andes up to 39 degrees South.

Farther north, the glacier made a limited advance into the High Andean Cordillera, the White Cordillera of Peru, and the Eastern Cordillera in Colombia. Around the coasts of both North and South America, the level of the oceans fell, uncovering vast sectors of the continental shelf. On the Atlantic side of South America sea level fell to about 150 metres below today's level. The glaciers began to retreat about 15,000 B.C. By about 9000 B.C. the ice had reached roughly its present-day positions.

Scientists are certain that humans did not originate in South America. Small groups of hunter-gatherers travelled south across the Central American isthmus, just as their ancestors had crossed the land bridge that today is open sea – the Bering Strait between North America and Asia. The earliest evidence of humans in South America dates from the end of the last glacial period.

At the end of the Ice Age, hunters armed with spears, clubs, and *bolas* (*left*) attack a herd of wild horses. The horse became extinct and reappeared in America only after many thousands of years, reintroduced by the Europeans.

# SOUTH AMERICA

## EARLY INHABITANTS— PALEOLITHIC HUNTERS AND GATHERERS

### Primitive Hunters

The exact dating of the oldest human settlements in South America is uncertain. Scientists know that by 11,000 B.C. humans had already settled in southern Chile and Patagonia. This means that they must have crossed the more northerly regions of the continent at a much earlier time. Discoveries made in Brazil and in the area of the Andes Mountains seem to confirm the existence in South America of groups of plant gatherers and hunters that had primitive stonecutting techniques.

The appearance of stone-tipped weapons indicates a world of advanced hunters. This was perhaps the result of a local technological revolution which occurred at one or more sites on the American continent. But it may have been a consequence of migratory movement of stone-using people from Siberia. The oldest South American settlements date from about 12,000 B.C. The Taima-Taima site in Venezuela (11,000 B.C.) produced the first barbed weapon heads, which subsequently spread throughout the Andes region. The Monteverde site, in southern Chile, contained the footprint of a child preserved in clay. At all recorded sites, there are traces of extinct animals, especially mastodons and horses. Remains of animals still thriving in South America were also found. These animals were hunted and exploited in various ways by the Paleo-Indians.

Around 9000 B.C., more highly skilled

The Pinturas River canyon, seen from the heights of Cueva de las Manos. The canyon is noted for its "negative" handprints, such as those shown on the left.

Guanacos are often depicted in rock paintings such as this example from Tarata, Peru.

*Below right:* **1)** A skull from Punin, Ecuador, is similar to those from other areas of the Andes, Brazil, and Patagonia. **2)** This double-edged razor found in the Los Toldos Grotto, Patagonia, is over 10,000 years old. **3)** Stone points with fishtail stems, or peduncles, were commonly used from 9000-7000 B.C.

groups of human beings appeared. They made spearheads of precise design. Like their predecessors, these people ranged as far as the southern tip of the continent. Typical artifacts are projectile points with an extended base in the form of a fishtail. Some points are fluted, similar to those of the Clovis points found in North America. The communities composing this Paleo-American culture hunted the last wild horses of the pampas of Patagonia.

## Hunters and Gatherers in the Andes Region

From about 8000 B.C., the Andes region was inhabited by people who used stone weapons to hunt various animals. But hunting was not their principal means of finding food. They were specialized gatherers, capable of living in a variety of ecological niches in the Andean plateau and valleys. These people often followed the seasonal movements of the animals. Hunting was probably only done in an organized way in summer on the mountain slopes.

This intensive hunting and gathering developed in the Andes region over a period of roughly 5,000 years. Two important cultural adaptations occurred here. Along the northern and central coast of Chile lived seafood gatherers and fishers. In the high Andes valleys lived the migratory hunter-gatherer-planters. Among these people were the originators of American agriculture.

## Rock Art

Since it is not possible to date rock painting found in northern and eastern Brazil, scientists maintain that the oldest known rock art in America was made by Patagonian hunters of the Tolden tradition. These pictures have simple geometrical elements. There are also images of guanacos (at times grouped with human figures) and of human hands. Llamas also appear in paintings by postglacial Andean hunters. These are found in Peru and Chile.

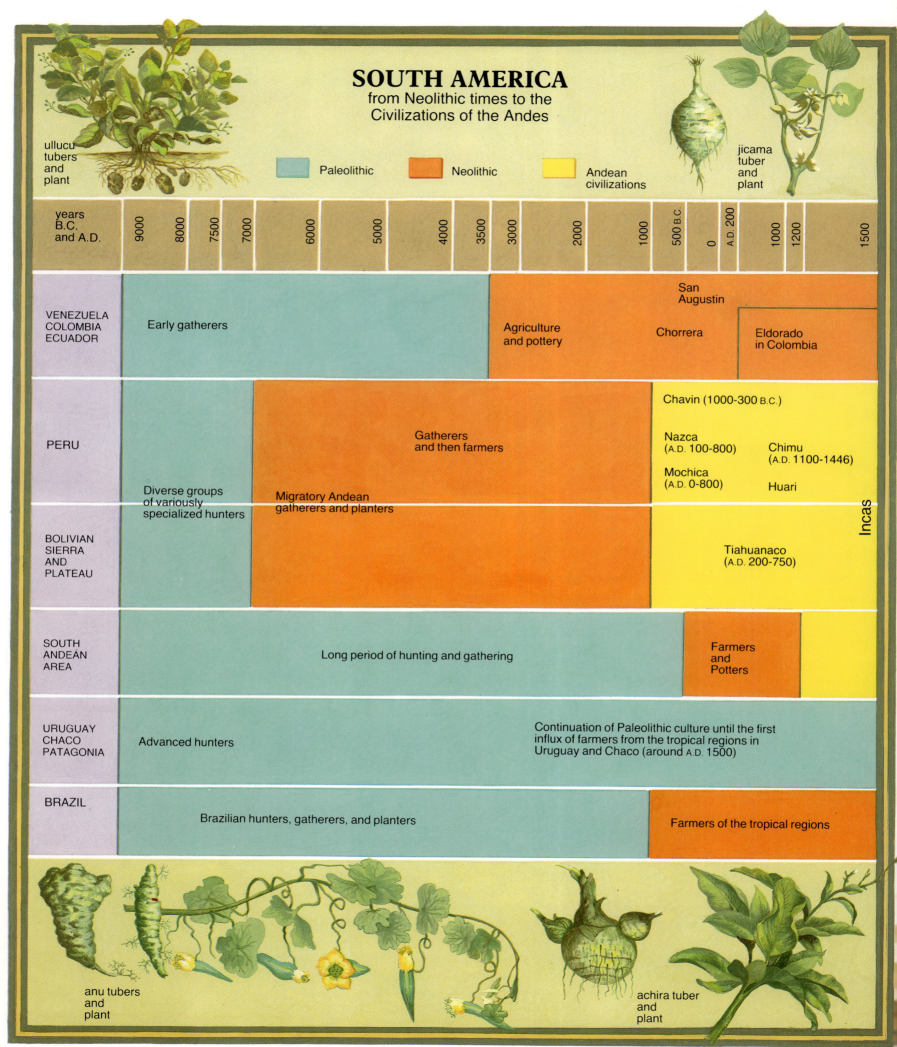

# EARLY FARMERS AND POTTERS

In the Andes region, agriculture began with the cultivation of various plants in widely separated areas. Around 7000 B.C., people in northern Peru cultivated beans and a variety of maize was grown in northwestern Argentina. Around 5900 B.C., maize appears as a crop on the northern coast of Chile. Somewhat later, traces of poroto beans were found at Pichasca. These sporadic indicators show that some hunter-gatherer groups, in the Andean tradition, practised a simple form of agriculture during a break in their seasonal migration. At the same time, humans began to domesticate the llama. However, that process took about 2,000 years.

Around 2500 B.C., another great innovation occurred. The cultivation of cotton made possible the development of the important Peruvian craft of weaving.

In this new cultural phase, villages multiplied and grew. The art of decoration of baskets and gourd vessels also developed. Stone products of this phase were rather clumsy. The axe was the predominant tool.

From about 2000 B.C., religious ideas were reflected in complex funeral rites and in the construction of temples in both the coastal and mountainous regions. The builders used squared stones held together with clay-based mortar. In some instances, the sacred enclosures were erected on top of one or two platforms.

in common use among at least two groups that were active around 3200 B.C. They lived at Puerto Hormiga, in the river region of northern Colombia, and at Valdivia, on the coast of Ecuador.

The Valdivia site is particularly interesting. After a phase characterized by local rough pottery, came a phase marked by splendid pottery with incised motifs, similar to the pottery of a contemporary Japanese culture known as Jomon. This suggests that here was not simply a culture of modest fishermen, as was once thought. Valdivia had a large religious complex called Real Alto. Real Alto had a large plaza surrounded by sacred mounds.

This container with its incised decorations was made from a large, hollowed-out gourd. (Huaca Prieta, Peru, 2000 B.C.)

This condor with a serpent on its breast is a decoration produced by applying a dye to cotton cloth. (Huaca Prieta, Peru, about 2000 B.C.)

These two ceramic statuettes were probably intended as fertility symbols. These are among the oldest-known pieces of South American pottery. (Valdivia, 3200-1800 B.C.)

From these starting points agriculture developed in the Andean and Peruvian regions. At the same time, new species of plants were used. Among these were amaranth, cucumbers and gourds, quinoa (pigweed, a cereal), and maize. People ate the tubers of the ullucu, anu, jicama, and achira plants. They also grew different varieties of potato, originally found wild. This entire process unfolded without the invention of pottery, as is common almost everywhere in agriculture's early stages.

## Origins and Spread of Pottery

The coastal areas of Colombia and Ecuador offer a different picture. There, clear traces of agriculture (including maize cultivation) can be traced back to 3000 B.C. Agriculture coexisted with a hunter-gatherer diet based on seafoods. Pottery techniques originated in this region. Crockery with incised decorations was

Over the centuries, the craft of pottery spread from this centre. Archaeological data for this spread is known in Venezuela, in the western Amazon Basin, around 2000 B.C. Other important sites were in the Lake Titicaca region (Peru/Bolivia) about 1200 B.C., and in northern Chile and northwestern Argentina around 500 B.C.

# THE NORTHERN ANDES

Highlighted on the map is the northern mountain region where the nations of Ecuador and Colombia are found today.

## Characteristics of the Region

The mountainous areas of Colombia and Ecuador and the Pacific coasts represent a link in the climatic and topographical chain between the Central American area and the Andean area proper. The landscape offers a contrasting panorama—a hot and humid coastal region, a Cordillerian region with basins and temperate valleys, and the wild eastern slope. This variety of landscapes accounts for the diversity of regional cultures, the development of which was influenced by the cultures of Central America and the Andes.

## Chorrera Pottery

In times of increasing trade, early Neolithic communities multiplied. Religion developed, and some villages were transformed into centres of worship. This tradition was continued by the Chorrera culture, the most important culture of Ecuador's "late development" period. This culture was known for the remarkable quality of its handmade painted pottery (1500-500 B.C.). Cultivation of maize underwent its greatest diffusion in the Guayas River basin.

## The Monuments of San Augustin

At San Augustin, a region near the source of the Magdalena River in southern Colombia, evidence of monumental religious architecture exists. San Augustin has been dated at around 500 B.C. Little is known of the people, their economy, or their social organization.

Ritual and burial centres were concentrated in groups arranged in a circular pattern extending roughly 50 kilometres. The culture produced monoliths that have only recently been discovered. These ancient stone structures were often found buried in the subsoil or beneath a tangle of vegetation. Their height varies from about 1 to 2.5 metres. Their rough symbolism is difficult to interpret. Among the various motifs is that of a man with cat-like features, sometimes wielding a weapon or symbolic instrument. There are unusual images of humans with "doubles"—sometimes an animal, sometimes a head with arms radiating outwards.

In the neighbouring region of Tierradentro lived people with cultural ties to San Augustin. Their sculpture was much simpler. However, they constructed great tombs with walls and roofs painted in complicated geometrical patterns. The semi-circular burial chambers are entered through a vertical shaft. The body of the deceased was surrounded by jars and other offerings.

*Left, and on the opposite page:* These two similar monoliths originally stood at the entrance to a megalithic temple. They represent a warrior with club in hand, his "double" hovering above his head. (San Augustin, Colombia) *Below:* Monolithic statues line the path leading to an underground temple in San Augustin.

*Opposite page on top:* This ceramic statuette is typical of Chorrera art, which reached its peak between the 900s and 500s B.C.

The plan (*left*) and cross section (*below*) show a temple hollowed out from the earth at Tierradentro, Columbia. Entrance was gained through a vertical shaft with stairs. The ceiling was supported by two pillars.

This gold raft is a replica of those used during the El Dorado ceremony, which was celebrated on Guatavita Lagoon.

## Gold: The Treasure of the Sun-God

At the beginning of the years A.D., various cultures developed in what is now Colombia. These people lived in villages but rarely formed larger, complex organizations. Following this was a period of regional development. People in this period generally had an advanced technology. They were sophisticated in the areas of arts and crafts. Their products included pottery that shows great variation in both form and decoration, small statues, and small replicas of curved-roof dwellings with large facades and single entrances. In some of these objects, one can see the influence of Central American art. This confirms that trade was carried on between Central and South America.

The highest development in the arts occurred among certain groups between about A.D. 500 and 1540. During this period, advanced techniques of working with gold were mastered. These techniques included moulding, soldering, hammering and alloying gold with copper, as well as relief work and filigree. The art objects are usually found in large cemeteries. They include vessels shaped like human and animal figures and various ornaments that were probably religious symbols.

Gold had no intrinsic economic value for these people. However, because of its colour and purity, it was considered to be a reflection of the sun, the supreme god. One legend tells of a hero who was reincarnated as a tribal chief. Part of the investiture ceremony involved sprinkling his body with powdered gold followed by a ritual voyage on a raft. This story gave rise to the legend of El Dorado, which so enthralled European explorers and treasure-seekers. One of the most important gold objects ever discovered in South America is connected with this legend: it is a small gold raft with human figures on board.

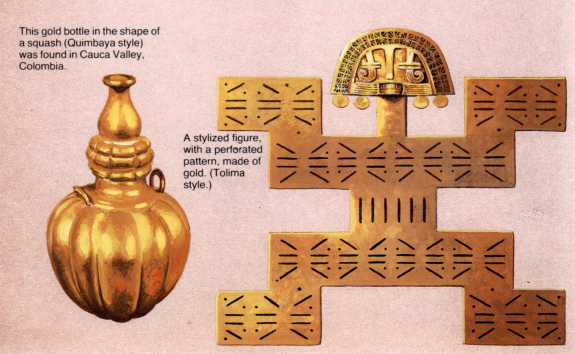

This gold bottle in the shape of a squash (Quimbaya style) was found in Cauca Valley, Colombia.

A stylized figure, with a perforated pattern, made of gold. (Tolima style.)

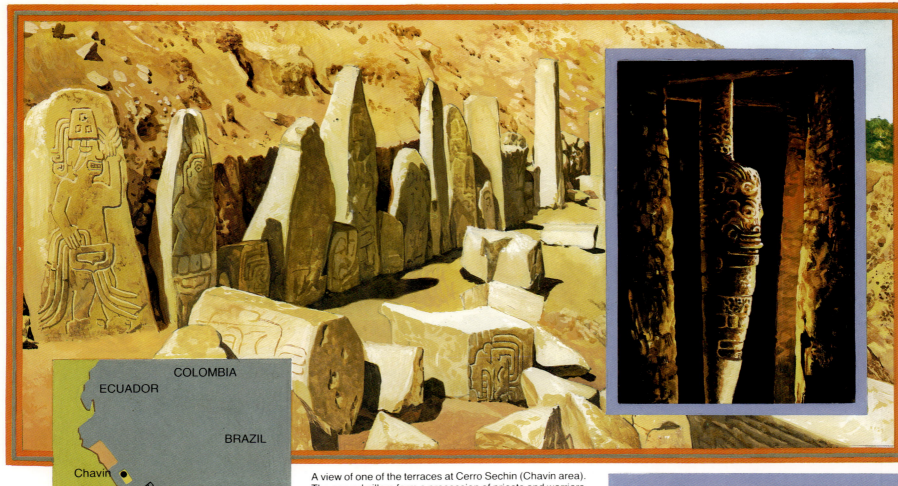

A view of one of the terraces at Cerro Sechin (Chavin area). The carved pillars form a procession of priests and warriors. The oldest part of the temple foundations dates from before 1000 B.C.

*In the inset:* The lanzon or lance of Chavin (900 B.C.) is a monolith 4 metres high embedded in the temple. It is decorated with a monster, half-man and half-cat. The lanzon was the centre of Chavin society and the link between heaven and earth.

Map of the Andean region. The Mochica culture is shown in orange; the Chavin culture in yellow; and the Nazca culture in blue.

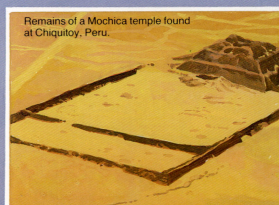

Remains of a Mochica temple found at Chiquitoy, Peru.

# ANDEAN CIVILIZATION

## The Chavin Culture (1000-300 B.C.)

South American cultural development reached its highest levels in what are now Peru and northern Bolivia. In these areas, over just a few centuries, a number of cult centres combined to form a community centred on an important temple complex called Chavin de Huantar. Its design blended elements from the coast and the jungle. The coast was symbolized by rectangular architecture with platforms. The jungle was characterized by decorations of jaguars, eagles, and serpents. The initial structure, which can be dated to 1000 B.C., had a series of interior galleries where initiation rites were probably performed and where offerings were placed. At the intersection of two interior galleries, there exists, still intact, a column in the form of a spear—the so-called *lanzon*.

The Chavin culture underwent a rapid expansion in the mountains and along the coast. The Chavin centres suggest a strict class system, influenced by the priest-class. From these centres developed towns and city-states, where the people displayed a high level of technical and artistic achievement. Archaeologists refer to this as the "classic" period. The economy was based on a fully developed agriculture. Irrigation was practised, and in mountainous regions, hillsides were terraced for cultivation. Other characteristics of these Andean centres were the concentration of population, the intensity of commerce, and the working of gold. Social stratification was complex. In time the government

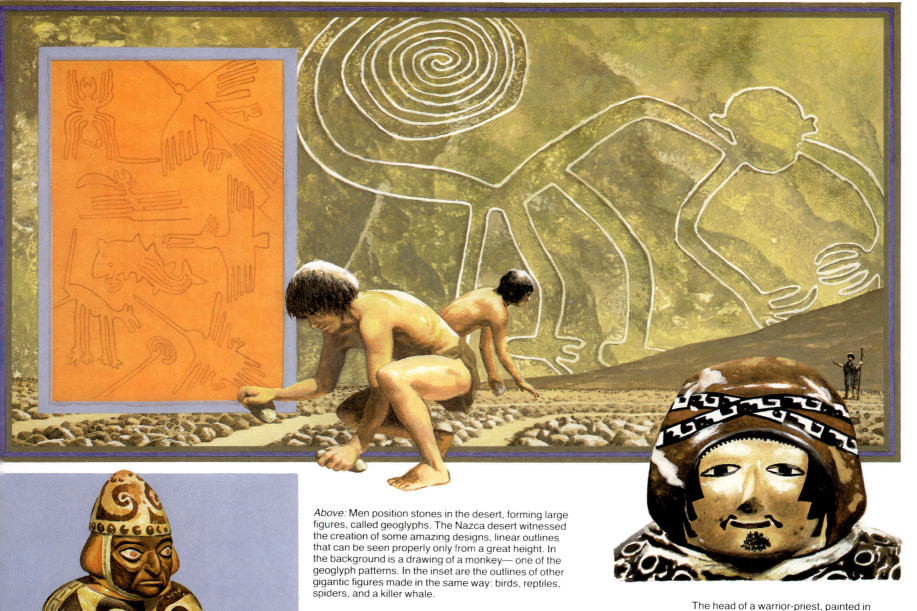

*Above:* Men position stones in the desert, forming large figures, called geoglyphs. The Nazca desert witnessed the creation of some amazing designs, linear outlines that can be seen properly only from a great height. In the background is a drawing of a monkey— one of the geoglyph patterns. In the inset are the outlines of other gigantic figures made in the same way: birds, reptiles, spiders, and a killer whale.

The head of a warrior-priest, painted in bright colours, is an example of Nazca pottery from the late A.D. 400s.

Ceramic figure of a kneeling warrior. The great skill needed to capture the human face and its expressions is one of the characteristics of Mochica art.

Terra-cotta statues depicting two fishermen in light reed canoes are examples of Mochica art (Totora).

of priests was replaced by a government of nobles and a monarchy, with the advent of a warrior class.

## The Nazca Culture (A.D. 100-800)

The Nazca culture began to develop on the south coast of Peru around A.D. 100. There people produced decorated pottery. Decorations ranged from realistic depictions of plants and animals to abstract, complicated symbolism.

Nazca religious activities usually took place in the open. Markings found on rocks seem to be references to stars and the heavens. The Nazcas made furrows in the rocky soil. Some of these furrows were linear and may have been ritual pathways. Other furrows, the famous "Nazca lines", were gigantic outlines of animals, startling when seen from the air.

## The Mochica Culture (A.D. 1-800)

The Mochica culture was centred in northern Peru. The Mochica developed an original architecture that utilized adobe (mud) bricks. The bricks were used for both dwellings and step-pyramids. The best examples are the Tombs of the Sun and the Moon, that face each other at the entrance to Moche Valley. The Mochica navigated along the coasts in boats made from reeds. They engaged in trade and occasionally warred against neighbouring peoples. It is through their pottery that these people are known. Because of its realistic decoration, they have been termed the "Greeks of America".

This painted wooden mask with eyes of seashells and silver, and hair of vegetable fibres comes from a tomb in the sacred city of Pachacamac.

A tapestry depicting a mythical bird or a butterfly, from Tiahuanaco and dating from after A.D. 1000.

This map shows settlements found along the coast and near the Peruvian mountains on the eve of the Inca domination. Yellow: Chimu kingdom (A.D. 1100-1466). Pink: Tiahuanaco kingdom (A.D. 200-750).

# ON THE EVE OF THE INCAS

## The Tiahuanaco Culture (A.D. 200-750)

About 20 kilometres southeast of Lake Titicaca, at an altitude of 3,800 metres, are the ruins of the first planned city in the Andes. Tiahuanaco was originally one of the many villages that arose near the lake, beginning in 1200 B.C. The inhabitants supported themselves by cultivating tubers and rice. They also kept sheep and llamas. By about A.D. 100, there were stone statues and feline symbols—an indirect reflection of the Chavin culture.

A hierarchy of priests held power. The inhabitants grew prosperous from farming and commerce. Caravans of llamas were used to carry on trade beyond the Andes regions. Local monuments included a great open rectangular enclosure, known as a kalasasaya, and a step-pyramid. The pottery was extremely well finished, and the most common form was a drum-shaped vessel.

The presence of a statue with a trophy head, in addition to weapons, hints more at sacrificial practices than at war. It provides evidence of worship of the human skull, which recurs in many prehistorical societies and is especially typical of the ethnology of the American continent.

Huari was a city in the central highlands of Peru. It was prominent from about A.D. 600-1000. In about A.D. 700 or 800, Huari expanded to southern and central Peru. In this process, Huari absorbed the ancient kingdom of Moche. Huari then became a model for city-states that survived the fall of that empire. Huari culture was first influenced by Nazca and then by Tiahuanaco, adopting the latter's religious symbolism and style. The Huari Empire ended by about A.D. 1000. In its place a number of smaller, local kingdoms developed. These included Colla, Chincha, Chancay, and Chimu.

## The Chimu Kingdom

Located in the valleys of Peru's arid northern coast, the Chimu kingdom gained control over the slopes of the Sierra. Its economy was founded on agriculture and commerce in various crafts. Its centre was Chan-Chan, an enormous urban complex. The buildings were barrack-like, rectangular, and each had its own temple and palace. The walls of unfired bricks displayed remarkable bas-reliefs, executed in a style inspired by textile art.

Chimu pottery continued the ancient tradition of making the handle in the form of a stirrup. It was no longer multi-coloured. It was deep grey or black and had a metallic brilliance, obtained through a technique of burnishing and firing. Another Chimu specialty was the art of working in precious metals. Utensils, necklaces, and statuettes of gold and silver were crafted by hand.

The Chimu kingdom was founded on military prowess and grew into a small empire. This kingdom was defended to the south by the fortress of Paramonga and by a wall that extended as far as the Andes. In spite of this, Chimu was conquered by the Incas around the middle of the 1400s.

*Above:* The city of Chan-Chan, the capital of the Chimu kingdom. The city consisted of large rectangular areas, each enclosed by a wall of unfired bricks, with a temple and palace on the inside.

*Opposite page, top:* Seen here are the Gate of the Sun and the remains of the great open rectangular enclosure at Tiahuanaco.

*Opposite page, bottom:* A llama caravan makes its way along the shore of Lake Titicaca, carrying goods to the city of Tiahuanaco.

*On the left:* Costume of an important person of the Chimu kingdom, reconstructed based on information from archaeological finds.

# THE INCA EMPIRE

The origins of the Inca Empire are surrounded in legend. It began as a small kingdom that, like neighbouring kingdoms, had broken away from the empire of Huari. In A.D. 1438, the Inca Yupanki rose to power. He was a great warrior and statesman who took the title of Pachacuti, or "he who opens a new era". Under his rule, the Incas expanded from their capital city of Cuzco. This city became one of the greatest cities of early America.

## The Three Conquerors

Inca traditions mention three sovereigns as the conquerors and organizers of the empire. In addition to being the first ruler, Pachacuti Inca Yupanki is also known for his reorganization of the empire on both political and social levels. His conquests included the areas of Peru closest to Cuzco and the Colla kingdom on Lake Titicaca. He was succeeded by his son, Tupac Inca Yupanki, who extended the empire to the central and southern coast of Peru, the southern Bolivian plateau, northwestern Argentina, and northern and central Chile. Huayna Capac, son of Tupac Inca Yupanki, enlarged and consolidated present-day Ecuador. There he established a second capital called Quito.

## The End of the Empire

The eldest son and successor to Huayna Capac, Huascar, did not succeed in holding

Map of the Inca Empire. Cuzco and three present-day national capitals are provided as reference points.

empire under PACHACUTI
empire under TUPAC
empire under HUAYNA CAPAC

*Left:* A plan of Macchu Pichu. Some of its features include: **1)** access stairway, **2)** terraced central esplanades, **3)** solar observatory, **4)** steep sloped terrace, and **5)** temple of the "Three Windows".

*Below:* Machu Picchu as it appears today. The alignment of the illustration and the plan are roughly the same. It is thus possible to locate the various parts of the city indicated on the plan, except for the access staircase.

the empire together. Civil war broke out in the empire when Huascar's cousin, Atahualpa, rose up against him and eventually defeated him in a bloody encounter.

By this time, the Incas faced a new foe—European invaders. A handful of Spaniards, led by Francisco Pizarro, were clever enough to take advantage of the confusion caused by the war. They imprisoned Atahualpa in 1532 and condemned him to death the following year. The advent of a new ruler and the founding of the Spanish city of Lima, on the central coast, marked the fall of the Inca Empire. Their traditions, however, persisted among many of the Indian groups of the region.

## Inca Culture

The Incas encapsulated 3,000 years of Andean technological and cultural development. Their originality consisted above all in the organization of their empire, one of the greatest in history. The Inca sovereign was at the centre of this system.

A widespread system of roads leading out from Cuzco and extending in all directions was dotted with cities, villages, and relay stations. These roads were used by men transporting goods on llamas, by armed troops, and by messengers known as *chasqui*. On the high southern hills, sacrificial rites were often celebrated in honour of the gods of sky and fertility.

The Incas were masters of monumental architecture. Their buildings are made of perfectly fitted, massive stone blocks. The fortress of Sacsayhuaman near Cuzco and the high mountain cities of Machu Picchu and Ollantaytambo are the best examples. An Inca city had terraces cut into the hillsides for crop-growing, irrigation canals, bridges, mines, and metalworking centres.

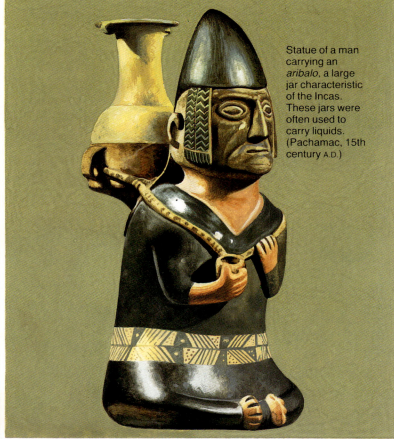

Statue of a man carrying an *aribalo*, a large jar characteristic of the Incas. These jars were often used to carry liquids. (Pachamac, 15th century A.D.)

*Above:* These pictures show scenes of Inca life, taken from documentary records made by Spanish conquistadors: **1)** sowing of maize, **2)** hoeing and weeding of maize, **3)** harvesting of maize, **4)** a woman weaving on a simple loom, **5)** a messenger, or chasqui, who travelled on foot, delivering messages by word of mouth.

*Right:* The governor is carried on a litter by his attendants into Cuzco.

# THE SOUTHERN ANDES

The Southern Andes area includes the semi-arid and arid regions that make up present-day Bolivia, northern Chile, northwest and midwest Argentina, and the central region of Chile. Here, after the ice ages, lived Andean hunter-gatherers. The pre-ceramic, agricultural period has no continuous characteristics, and little is known about it. The use of pottery began here at a later date than in Peru. Neolithic cultures borne by groups arriving from areas farther north began about 500 B.C. in some regions of northwest Argentina and northern Chile. In other regions, this did not occur until three centuries later.

## First Farmers and Potters (500 B.C.-A.D. 600)

Groups of farmers and llama breeders, skilled in the basic principles of irrigation, settled in villages, populating the Andean and sub-Andean regions. Other groups settled in the forests of eastern Bolivia and the westernmost belt of the Chaco plain. There were noticeable differences between these groups, especially in environmental adaptation and in their diverse pottery styles. On the Pacific coast of Chile, fishermen and seafood gatherers settled.

In the valleys of northwest Argentina, most villages consisted of circular dwellings, arranged in loose groupings. In some villages, though, the dwellings were set around a central circular plaza.

## Middle Period (A.D. 600-900)

There is no record of important changes in the technical-economic aspects of the culture. However, two regions show signs of the direct or indirect influence of the great artistic and cultural centre of Tiahuanaco. The first region is San Pedro de Atacama. Found in the northern desert territory of Chile, San Pedro is the source of various items of household art, clothing, flutes, small vases, and other wooden objects.

Similar influences from the plateaus led to the birth of La Aguada culture in northwestern Argentina. La Aguada culture destroyed or absorbed many others and came to be the most significant element in the region. Its society was headed by warrior-priests. These priests are often depicted, while in trances, with the symbol of a dragonlike cat. The use of bronze is evident from such objects as ritual axes and various types of discs or breastplates. These pieces show a god flanked by two cats, a figure also found in Bolivia.

## The Late Period (A.D. 1000-1550)

After a phase marked by migrations of people from the tropical forests, a number of local groups began to develop. The advances represented by this period consisted of greater population density. In large part, these people were concentrated in settlements, called *pucara*. Many of these semi-urban settlements were heavily fortified. There were also a greater development of agricultural irrigation, a more complex social structure, and a more consistent development of bronze-working techniques. These new methods were used in the manufacture of tools, weapons, and ritual objects.

The southern Andean area is rich in rock paintings (especially in northern Argentina and Chile) and carvings (in the western regions). The paintings were mainly the work of the farming and pot-making peoples. The main subjects of this rock art were animals and abstract symbols, presumably linked to rites performed by the priests.

## Inca Rule (A.D. 1475-1535)

The expansion of the Inca Empire into the southern Andes was short-lived and did not dramatically alter local cultures. The Incas opened new roads across territories remote from old towns. Their main interest was in mining, over which they probably held a monopoly, and in trade routes with Chile, the source of minerals and certain foods. The most remarkable remains of this period are the sanctuaries of the High Cordillera as much as 6,700 metres above sea level.

A flute player from Chile.

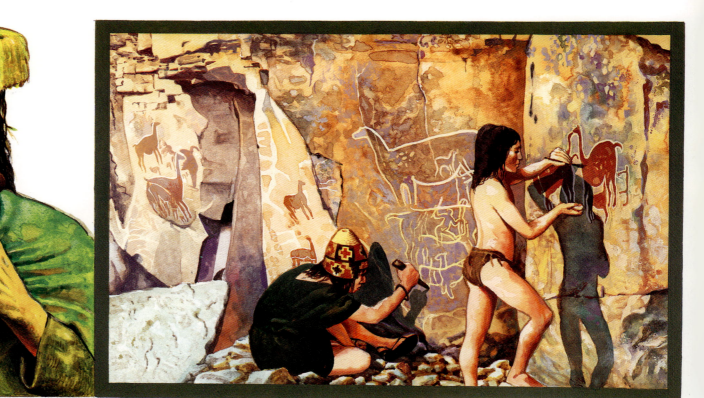

Two men carve and paint the images of guanacos on a cave wall at Taira in the Loa River valley, Chile. Rock art is a feature of this area.

A view of one part of the Pucara at Tilcara includes the llama pens.

*Left:* **1)** A wooden tablet shows the influence of Tiahuanaco in its decorative patterns. **2-3)** Nasal tubes, carved from wood, were used to inhale substances. (Atacama, Chile)

- Taira
- Tilcara

Atacama

- La Aguada
- Belén
- Coquimbo

This bronze plaque depicts human figures, perhaps gods, flanked by two cats. (La Aguada, Argentina)

A black vase carved with the image of a mythical animal, half-dragon and half-cat. (La Aguada)

This gold statuette with well-preserved cloak and feathered headdress was found in an Inca mountain sanctuary at Cerro Gallan, Argentina.

A toki, or bronze ritual axe, from the Argentinian northwest.

This funeral urn is decorated with a human face, probably that of the deceased. Urns of this Belen type come from northwest Argentina.

This rock carving depicts a large head in the form of a mask. (El Molle culture, A.D. 200-700, El Encanto Valley, Coquimbo, Chile)

Population patterns and cultural influences from 2000 B.C. to A.D. 100.

Population patterns and cultural influences from A.D. 100 to A.D. 500.

Along a riverbend in the Amazon forest, a group of Indians, having arrived by canoe, has begun to build a village. The huts are made of wood and, in the area where trees have been felled and the underbrush burned away, the people are planting manioc, using digging sticks. To the right, two boys are using friction by rotating a stick on top of a dry branch in order to start a fire. In the foreground, two women grate manioc tubers to make flour. Behind them, other women are weaving reed baskets. On the river, fish are being caught with a harpoon.

# People of the Caribbean, the Amazon Basin, and Eastern and Southern Brazil

Between the eastern slopes of the Andes and the Atlantic Ocean lies a vast area of the South American continent that did not reach the cultural level attained in other regions. In some cases, there were groups acquainted with agriculture and pottery. In other cases, hunters and gatherers persisted, as in the forests of southeastern Brazil.

## The Caribbean Basin

The Caribbean Basin covers the northern region of Venezuela and the islands of the Caribbean. Direct influences from the northern Andean region were felt here. One example was the *barrancoid* culture in the area around the Orinoco Delta. Pottery painted with complex decorative patterns was made here between 1000 to 500 B.C. It resembled the pottery of northern Colombia.

Other local traditions developed, whose existence was based on cultivation and in part on fishing and the gathering of seafood. Some groups were skilled in seafaring and settled over a large part of the Antilles. Their descendants were the Caribs, one of the first Native Americans to come in contact with Europeans.

## Equatorial Forest and Tropical Savanna Regions

The Amazon River has the largest river basin in the world. The Amazonian rainforest was largely avoided by early hunters. Once the

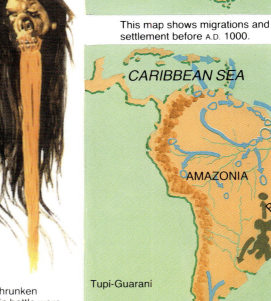

*Above:* Two examples of *tsanta*, or shrunken heads. The heads of enemies taken in battle were shrunk and preserved as trophies by the Jivaro Indians in the Amazon region of Ecuador. *Top:* This curved stone axe comes from the Paraná River regions and dates from about 5000 B.C.

This map shows migrations and settlement before A.D. 1000.

This map shows migrations and settlement between A.D. 1000 and 1520.

Neolithic mode of life became established in the western mountain regions, scattered groups broke off and migrated. These migrants took advantage of river currents, and eventually settled down at favourable sites along the river's banks. Recent archaeological excavations suggest the very early existence (4000 B.C.) of peoples already familiar with pottery. Next came the Ananatuba tribe (1000 B.C.) living on the island of Marajo near the mouth of the Amazon.

Like the Ananatubas, other groups of farmers spread outwards along the Amazon River basin and along Brazil's northern coast. Because stone suitable for tool-making was scarce, except for occasional outcrops, their tools were made of wood and other perishable materials. These people lived in isolated villages and, in addition to growing crops such as manioc and maize, lived by fishing, hunting, and gathering.

Multi-coloured pottery was made in the low Amazon River basin around A.D. 1000. This pottery included funerary urns decorated with geometrical symbols. There was an increase in the number of villages along the waterways. The dead were buried in large mounds of earth, some more than 50 metres in diameter. There is also evidence of the beginning of social stratification. Certain Amazon tribes engaged in skull worship and headhunting. The most notable such trophies are the shrunken heads of the Jivaro Indians of eastern Ecuador.

## The Tupi-Guarani Expansion

A tribe of Amazon origin, the Tupi-Guarani, expanded to the south, from about A.D. 500. This tribe was centred mainly in eastern Bolivia and Paraguay, and along the entire Brazilian coast in the east.

The Guarani, whose cultural and linguistic influence is still evident on present-day Amerindians, were known for a varied pottery. This included decorated funerary urns sometimes painted and sometimes ridged, with raised areas created by pressing the wet clay with the fingers. Trade, as well as tribal migrations, caused this pottery to be found from the central Amazon to the Parana River delta. A widely used tool was the polished stone axe, fixed to a long wooden handle. The villages consisted of communal long houses surrounded by a circular fence that provided defence during frequent tribal conflicts.

The southern part of South America: now occupied by the modern states of Uruguay, Argentina and Chile.

# THE CHACO, THE PAMPA, AND URUGUAY

The western part of the Plata River Basin consists of a flat plain partially subject to flooding. The northern part between the Parana and the Salado rivers is known as the Chaco, which means "hunting area". The temperate plain which extends farther south is called the Pampa or "plain devoid of trees".

## The Pampa and Uruguay

In the eastern section, corresponding to the present-day Republic of Uruguay and to the southern part of the Rio Grande do Sul (Brazil), the countryside is rolling, marked by only occasional flat areas. Unlike the Chaco region, this area shows much evidence of its past inhabitants. The people who lived here were hunters who moved through the region leaving many stone objects behind them. The most typical items were spear points or arrowheads with small barbs. Also used were throwing stones or *bolas*, tents, and leather cloaks. The cloaks were sometimes decorated with geometrical patterns that recall the cliff paintings found in southern Uruguay. These natives, called the Charruas during the Spanish era, are considered to be related to the Tehuelches of Patagonia.

Not far away, in northern Uruguay, a population of gatherers survived until shortly before the arrival of the Europeans. They were characterized by a type of stone flake tool known as catalan, that appears to have been absorbed by the Charruas. Also in the humid Pampa of Argentina, a new technology and economy appeared. Along with the traces of general hunting, there is evidence of sporadic migrations of more specialized hunters from the Andean and perhaps the Patagonian region.

## The Chaco

Archaeological information on the Chaco is

Life in a village in the Chaco region. The huts are built of branches and reeds. At the left, a man with tubular pipe in hand, keeps an eye on food as it cooks. Other men leave on a hunt carrying bows and arrows. Leaning against a tree trunk in the foreground are fishing nets and hollow gourds for holding water. Some children play with bows. A fisherman returns with his catch (*right*). In the foreground (*right*), a storage platform raised above ground is used to store grain and other foods.

A Chaco Indian wears a typical mask.

*Left:* Flint spearpoints such as those shown far left were used by Uraguayan hunters. Hunters in the Chaco used wooden arrowheads.

Funeral urns of painted terra-cotta were used by the Guarani who settled along the mouth of the Paraná River.

scarce because many tools were made of perishable materials. The life of the hunters, who roamed this region until the Spanish conquest, probably did not differ much from that of their better-known descendants, the Pilagas, Tobas, and Matacos. These tribes are known for their large wooden huts with straw roofs, built in forest openings. In addition to hunting and gathering, fishing was very important to the peoples of the Chaco.

## The Guarani Penetration

The last ethnic movement in this area is that of the Guarani. These river navigators settled along the banks of the Uruguay and Parana rivers shortly before the Spanish arrived. The most important group, studied in depth by archaeologists, had settled in the area of the Parana Delta and on the southwest coast of Uruguay. It is here, for example, that typical funerary urns were found.

The Guarani exerted their influence over the native Charruas, especially with regard to language and hunting customs. A number of separate groups settled in the heart of the Chaco, especially in regions near the eastern slopes of the Andes. The best artifacts produced consisted of painted pottery made by the tribes that settled in the Chaco. Other tribes produced masks of wood and feathers used in seasonal ceremonies. These tribes adapted so well to the subtropical environment typical of the Chaco that they abandoned agricultural practices and reverted to hunting and gathering.

# SOUTHERN CHILE, PATAGONIA, AND TIERRA DEL FUEGO

## The Araucanians

The Maule River, located at the extreme southern border of the Incan presence, can also be considered as the southern border of the Andean cultural area. The territory farther to the south was, and in part still is, the land of the Mapuche, or Araucanian, people. These people developed from ancient populations of hunters, seafood gatherers, and groups of farmer-potters who arrived from central Chile between the 400s and 900s A.D. They adapted to a humid climate and a wooded environment, partly retaining their old hunting and gathering activities.

south of the Limay and Negro rivers, were descendants of Ice Age hunters. These people specialized in hunting guanaco. Some time during their development, they added the use of bow and arrows to that of the spear and bolas. Around A.D. 1700, some groups began to use pottery to a limited extent. The harsh environment and climate of the region, however, prevented agriculture from coming into practice. Farming could not be carried out without a complex irrigation system. Housing among the Tehuelche and the Ona of Tierra del Fuego consisted of leather tents, supported by wooden posts. The people wore clothes

8000 B.C., immediately after the retreat of the glaciers. There is important evidence of their religious ceremonies, during which the men, completely naked in spite of the hostile climate, painted their bodies and covered their faces with large conical masks.

## The Canoeros

The wide, fanlike spread of islands which extends into the Pacific Ocean opposite the southern coast of Chile was populated by people called Canoeros. These people had adapted to the maritime environment. They lived in huts built on the coast and on the

At the southern extremity of South America are Patagonia and Tierra del Fuego.

Two Araucanian women in front of a ruca, which is a house with a straw roof.

## The Pehuenche

The Pehuenche of Argentina were a people adapted to the mountainous environment south of Mendoza and in the neighbouring province of Neuquen. Sixteenth-century chroniclers describe the traditions of these gatherers and nomadic shepherds. In addition to hunting and vegetable gathering, these people are also known for their use of rock salt and their huge cliff carvings in the rocky regions north of Neuquen and in the surrounding Chilean valleys.

## The Tehuelche

The Tehuelche, who settled in Patagonia

made from animal skins. Hunting was important, so these people migrated with their prey to some extent. In the mesetas (plateaus), it is still possible to find the tent supports and stone stockades that these people used during hunting expeditions.

## The Ona

The Ona were inhabitants of the northern plains of Tierra del Fuego. Their way of life remained unchanged for a long time. At some unknown date, their predecessors arrived across the sea from the northern coast of the Strait of Magellan. In ancient times, other groups had crossed that same stretch around

edges of the forested interior. Their main occupations were the gathering of molluscs along the shore and the harpoon-hunting of seals from canoes.

Groups of Canoeros were already present around 4000 B.C., and they continued to live by fishing for a thousand years. Around 2000 B.C., they also practised land hunting, mainly using bone harpoons. But these inhabitants of the far south of the continent disappeared after the arrival of the Europeans. Many fell victim to diseases brought by the Europeans.

A Tehuelche Indian wearing a colourful garment known as a quillango and carrying a bolas.

Bolas stones. Tied together with a cord and spun around, they make a very accurate and dangerous throwing weapon.

A ritual stone axe decorated with magical carvings.

In Patagonia, a family group of Ona Indians make arrows beneath the toldo, a shelter made of branches and animal skins.

This carved wooden head was part of a ritual totem used by the Araucanian Indians.

A canoe used by the Canoeros.

Bone harpoons such as these were used by the Canoeros.

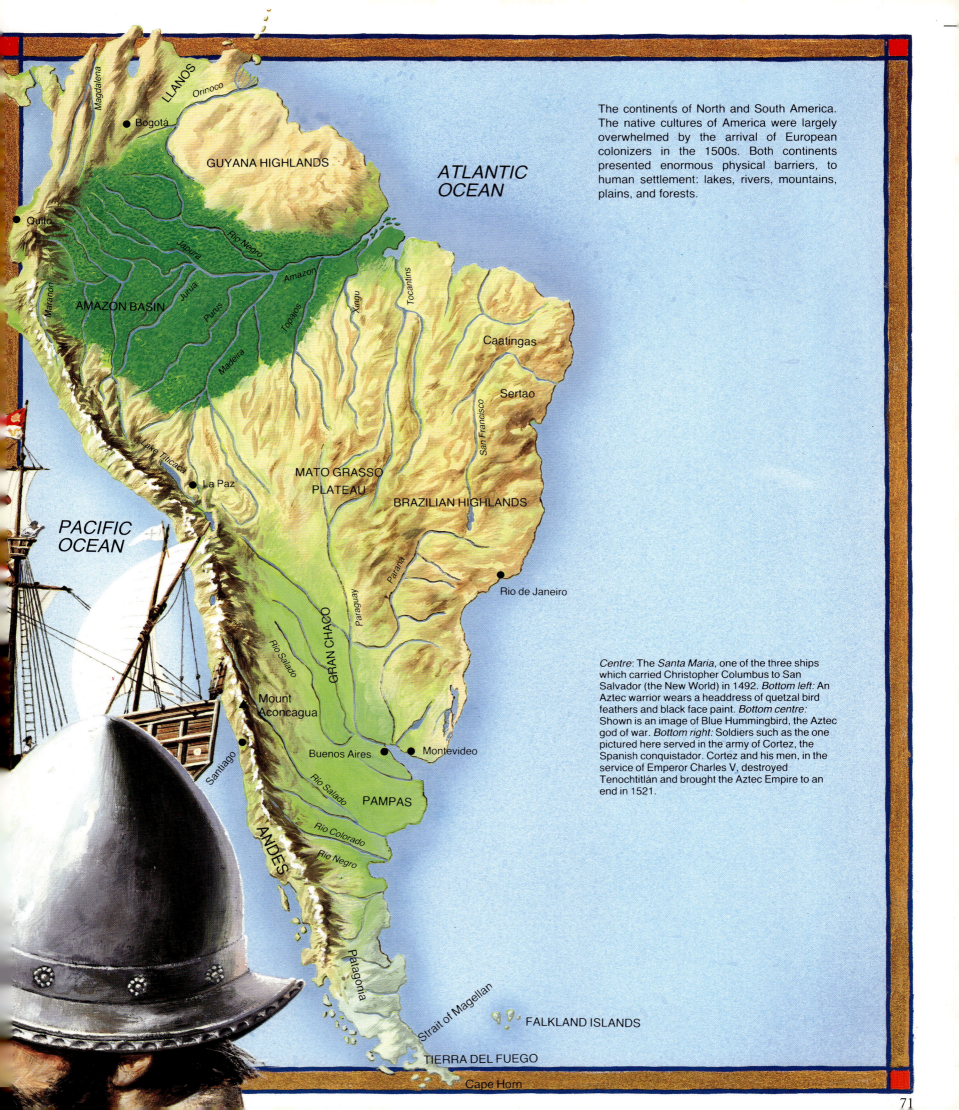

The continents of North and South America. The native cultures of America were largely overwhelmed by the arrival of European colonizers in the 1500s. Both continents presented enormous physical barriers, to human settlement: lakes, rivers, mountains, plains, and forests.

*Centre*: The *Santa Maria*, one of the three ships which carried Christopher Columbus to San Salvador (the New World) in 1492. *Bottom left*: An Aztec warrior wears a headdress of quetzal bird feathers and black face paint. *Bottom centre*: Shown is an image of Blue Hummingbird, the Aztec god of war. *Bottom right*: Soldiers such as the one pictured here served in the army of Cortez, the Spanish conquistador. Cortez and his men, in the service of Emperor Charles V, destroyed Tenochtitlán and brought the Aztec Empire to an end in 1521.

# GLOSSARY

**agriculture:** the processes and activities associated with farming; the work of planting seeds, producing crops, and rearing animals.

**animal husbandry:** breeding and caring for domesticated animals.

**anthropomorphism:** attributing human qualities to animals and objects.

**aqueduct:** a pipe system used to transport water from a distant place.

**archaeology:** the science that studies the remains of human activities—objects, tools, buildings, and works of art.

**architecture:** the process or profession of designing buildings of all types.

**arid:** dry; devoid of moisture or humidity.

**artifact:** any object made or crafted by human hands.

**artisan:** a skilled craftsperson.

**astronomy:** the study of stars and planets.

**barren:** sterile, unable to reproduce or bear fruit.

**basin:** all the land drained by a river and its branches. Water collects near a basin to form lakes.

**caravan:** a group of people travelling together, often through a desert.

**ceramics:** objects made of clay that are moulded into shape and baked in an oven.

**citadel:** a fortress or place of safety.

**codices:** long strips of tanned animal hides, arranged in accordion folds, used to keep the records of the Mixtec Indians. Codices contained narrative accounts of genealogies, marriages, military conquests, and so on.

**continent:** one of the principal land masses of the earth. Africa, Antarctica, Asia, Europe, North America, South America, and Australia are regarded as continents.

**cult:** a specific type of religious worship, with its own particular rules and ceremonies.

**cultivate:** to prepare land for the planting and growing of crops.

**decade:** a period of ten years.

**deciduous:** trees which shed their leaves each year during certain seasons.

**deity:** a god; a being who possesses a divine nature.

**diverse:** possessing different or various qualities; having unlike elements.

**domesticate:** the process of taming wild animals in order to use them for different purposes.

**earthworks:** huge structures of mounded earth constructed by Indians in the southeast region of North America.

**ecology:** the relationship between organisms and their environment. The science and study of ecology is extremely important as a means of conserving all the forms of life on earth.

**environment:** the circumstances or conditions of a plant or animal's surroundings. The physical and social conditions of an organism's environment influence its growth and development.

**equator:** an imaginary circle around the earth, equally distant at all points from both the North Pole and the South Pole.

**evolution:** a gradual process in which something changes into a different and usually more complex or better form. Groups of organisms may change with the passage of time so that descendants differ physically from their ancestors.

**excavate:** to make a hole or cavity in by digging; to form by hollowing out; to uncover or expose by digging.

**exotic:** strange or different; foreign.

**extinction:** the process of destroying or extinguishing. Many species of plant and animal life face extinction either because of natural changes in the environment or those caused by the carelessness of humans.

**fauna:** the animals that live and thrive in a specific environment at a specific period in time. The fauna of any place on earth is determined by the ability to adapt to and thrive in the existing environmental conditions.

**fertile:** rich in natural resources; able to produce and/or reproduce.

**flora:** the plants that grow in a specific environment at a specific period of time. The earth's flora varies from place to place.

**fossil:** a remnant or trace of an organism of a past geologic age, such as a skeleton or leaf imprint, embedded in some part of the earth's crust. Scientists search for fossils as a way of learning about past life.

**glaciers:** gigantic moving sheets of ice. Ice sheets covered great areas of the earth in an earlier time, notably during the ice ages.

**Haab:** the solar and civil calendar of the Maya Indians that included 365 days.

**harpoon:** a spearlike weapon with a barbed head used to hunt whales, seals, and large fish.

**herbivore:** an animal that eats plants. Horses and deer are herbivores.

**hieroglyphic:** a type of writing, as used by ancient Egyptians, in which certain signs and symbols (instead of letters) represent words.

**humid:** containing a large amount of water or water vapour; damp. Warm air currents floating through coastal areas produce a humid climate.

**hydraulic:** operated by the movement and force of liquid; operated by the pressure created where a liquid is forced through a tube.

**hypothesis:** a theory based on available supporting evidence.

**immigrate:** to move into a new region or country.

**implement:** a tool or utensil used to perform some specific activity.

**irrigate:** to carry or deliver water to dry land by artificial means such as tunnels or ditches.

**kivas:** ritual structures of the Pueblo Indians, resembling pithouses.

**lava:** melted rock that flows from an erupting volcano.

**lunar:** having to do with the moon and its changing phases.

**mammoth:** an extinct type of large, hairy elephant with curved tusks.

**migrate:** to move from place to place in search of food and shelter. Migration usually revolves around seasonal changes.

**mollusc:** any of a large group of animals having soft bodies enclosed in hard shells. Snails, oysters, and clams are molluscs.

**monarch:** the primary ruler of a state or kingdom, such as a king or queen.

**monolith:** something carved or formed from a single stone block.

**mural:** a large picture or scene painted on or attached to a wall.

**nomad:** a member of a tribe or people having no permanent home, but roaming about constantly in search of food and shelter.

**oasis:** area in a desert with a below-ground reservoir of water that allows the growth of trees and other plants.

**obsidian:** black, glasslike rock used in making small tools and ornaments.

**perishable:** likely to spoil or rot, as wooden or cloth artifacts do in hot, moist climates.

**petroglyphs:** stone carvings made by some peoples of early North America.

**pirogue:** a type of boat or canoe made from a hollowed-out tree trunk or log.

**pithouse:** a house made by digging a deep hole in the ground and then covering the top with matting or bark.

**plateau:** an elevated and more or less level expanse of land.

**plumage:** the feathers of a bird.

**portico:** a porch or covered walkway.

**precipitation:** water droplets that are condensed in the earth's atmosphere to form rain, sleet, or snow.

**primitive:** of or existing in the beginning or earliest times; uncivilized.

**prosperous:** having good fortune; well to do, successful.

**ritual:** a system of ceremonies or procedures, especially with regard to religious worship.

**sanctuary:** a place of peace or safety; a haven or place of rest; a special building set aside for holy worship.

**sarcophagus:** a large tomb, usually decorated or inscribed.

**shaman:** a medicine man or holy man of certain Indian tribes in the Americas; a magician.

**solar:** of or having to do with the sun or the sun's energy.

**species:** a specific type or class of plant or animal.

**subjugate:** to conquer and force into servitude or slavery.

**temperate:** a climate that is neither very cold nor very hot, but moderate.

**terrace:** a shelf, or level stretch of land, cut into a hillside.

**theocracy:** a type of government in which priests have priority and rule the state.

**tributary:** a small river or stream that usually flows into and is eventually part of a larger one.

**tuber:** a plant whose fruit develops and grows under the ground.

**tundra:** the immense, frozen plains of the Arctic and Antarctic.

**Tzolkin:** the religious calendar of the Maya Indians that included 260 days.

**urn:** a large vase or receptacle.

**valley:** a space of low land between hills or mountains often with a stream flowing through it.

**vessel:** a bowl, pot, or other receptacle used for holding or containing something.

# INDEX

## A

Acatl Topiltzin, 36
Adena culture, 20
adobe houses, 12
Agro-Ceramic period, 62
Aconcagua, 4
alloys, 43, 55
amaranth, 53
Americas
   discovery of, 4-5
   geographical features, 4
   oldest inhabitants, 6
   (see also Mesoamerica, North America, and South America)
Ananatuba, 65
Anasazi, 12-13, 14-15
Andes Mountains, 4, 50
animals
   domestication of, 12-13, 53
   in art, 11, 18, 20, 22-23, 25, 57, 62
*Annals of Cuauhitlán*, 36
Appalachian Mountains, 4, 18
aqueducts, 37
Araucanians, 68
Archaic, 8
Archaic people, 8-9, 12, 18, 20, 24
art
   of Andes region, 54-55, 56-57
   of Mississippian people, 22-23
   of North America, 11
   of Olmecs, 40-41
   rock painting, 26-27, 51, 62
   Teotihuacan, 33
astronomy, 45
Atahualpa, 61
atlatl, 28
Aztecs, 37, 39, 48

## B

bajareque temple, 32
Basketmaker period, 14
basketmaking (see crafts)
bolas, 66
burial rites, 11, 13, 20, 25, 31, 42, 43, 54

## C

caciquates, 45
calendar, 42, 45
Canadian Shield, 4
Canoeros, 68
Caracol, 47
Caribs, 64
Castillo, 47
catalan, 66
cenote, 47
ceremony, 14, 19, 22, 31
chacmol, 37
Chac Mool, 47
Chaco Canyon, 14
Chalchiuhtlicue, 33
Charruas, 66
chasqui, 61
Chavin culture, 56-57
Chavin de Huantar, 56
Chenes style, 46, 47
Chichen Itza, 46-47
Chimalma, 36
Chimu kingdom, 59
Chorrera culture, 54
citadel, 34-35
Classic period (in Mesoamerica), 28-29
Classic period, (in North America), 12
clothing, 21, 31
Clovis culture, 6
coastal regions, 4
codices, 43, 45
Cojico, 43
Colonial period, 12
Colorado House, 47
Columbus, Christopher, 5
crafts, 12-13, 18, 20, 25, 28, 30-31, 42-43, 53, 58-59
cremation, 20
Cuicuilco, 32-33

## D

Dainzu, 43
Danger Cave, Utah, 8
de Soto, Hernando, 22
deities, 33, 37

deserts, 4
draught animals, 22

# E

earthworks, 18-19, 22
ecosystems, 26
El Dorado, 55
Eric the Red, 5
Ericsson, Leif, 5
Eskimos, 5, 24-25

# F

farming, 12-13, 22, 49, 52-53
fishing, 10, 51
fire, use of, 28
fjords, 10
Four Corners region, 12

# G

gathering, 8-9, 17, 28, 51, 52
geoglyphs, 57
glaciation, 6, 27, 50
Grave Creek Mound, 20
grave goods, 20, 43
Great Basin, 8
Great Serpent Mound, Ohio, 20-21
"Greeks of America", 57

# H

Haab, 45
head-hunting, 65
hieroglyphics, 41, 42
Hohokam, 12-13
*Homo sapiens*, 5, 6, 50
Hopewell culture, 20
Huari, 59
Huascar, 60
Huayana Capac, 60
Huehueteotl, 33, 37
Huitzilopochtli, 37

hunting, 6, 11, 16-17, 20, 24-25, 28, 50-51, 52
  bison, 16-17
  caribou, 24, 26-27
  guanaco, 68
  seal, 24-25

# I

Ice Age, 6, 50
igloo, 25
Incas, 60-61
Indian, 5
Indian Knoll, Kentucky, 19
Inuit, 24-25
Ipiutak culture, 24-25
irrigation methods, 56
Itzá, 47

# J

jaguar (as symbol), 31, 40-41
Japanese Current, 10
Jivaro Indians, 65
Jomon period, 53

# K

kalasasaya, 59
kiva, 14

# L

La Aguada culture, 62
language, 5, 12
Late period, 62
Late Prehistoric period, 22
lodge, 17

# M

Major Temple, 37
Matacos, 66
Maya, 44-45, 48

Mayan cities, styles of, 46
Meadowcroft Shelter, 7, 20
Mesa Verde, 14
Mesoamerica, 28-49
  early inhabitants, 28
metalworking, 20, 43, 62
metals, 20, 55
Middle period
  (Andes regions of South America), 62
migration, human, 6-7, 9, 26, 48, 50
Mimbres (Mogollon subgroup), 13
Mississippian people, 22
Mixcoatl, 36
Mixtecs, 43
Mochica culture, 57
Mogollon, 12-13
monolith, 54
Monte Alban, 42
Monticula J, 42
mosaics, 43
mound building, 20
mountains, 4

# N

Nauhyotzin, 37
Nazca culture, 57
nomadic people, 28, 37
Norsemen (see Viking)
North America, 6-27
  Arctic, 24-25
  early inhabitants, 6-7
  Great Plains, 16-17
  intermountain area, 8-9
  Northeast Woodland, 20-21, 22-23
  Northwest Coast, 10-11
  Southeast, 18-19
  Southwest, 12-13, 14-15
  subarctic, 26-27
  West Coast, 8-9
numbers, 42, 45
Nuns Temple, 47

# O

Oecihuatl, 37

Olmecs, 40-41
Ometecuhtli, 37
Ona, 68

# P

Pachacuti Inca Yupanki, 60
Palenque style, 46
Paleo-Indians, 8, 12, 18
Pehuenche, 68
pelota, 48
petroglyphs, 11
Pilagas, 66
piñon pine tree, 8-9
Pioneer period, 12
pithouse, 11, 13, 14
Pizarro, Francisco, 61
plants, domestication of, 19, 28
Pleistocene epoch, 5, 6, 16
Plumed Serpent (see Quetzalcóatl)
pok-a-tok, 48
populations, human, 12, 18, 26
post-classic period, 28-29
pottery (see crafts)
Poverty Point, 18-19
pre-classic period, 28-29
pucara, 62
Pueblo Bonito, 14-15
Pueblo I period, 14
Pueblo II period, 14
Pueblo III period, 14
Pueblo IV period, 14
Pueblo V period, 14
Pueblos (Indians), 14
pueblos, 14-15
Pyramid of Niches, 49
Pyramid of the Moon, 33, 34-35
Pyramid of the Sun, 33, 34-35
pyramids, 13, 32-33

# Q

Quetzalcóatl, 33, 36-37
Quito, 60

## R

Real Alto, 53
religion, 32, 41, 48
Remojadas culture, 48
Rio Bec style, 46

## S

San Jose Mogote, 43
savannas, 4, 64
sculpture (see art)
"Second I," 54
seafaring, 27
Sedentary period, 12
Serpent Rain Cloud, 33
shaman, 30
snake (as symbol), 31
Snaketown (Arizona), 12
society, organization of, 5, 22, 37, 56
solar energy, 14
South America, 50-69
  Amazon Basin, 64-65
  Brazil, 64-65
  Caribbean Basin, 64-65
  Chaco, the, 66-67
  Chile, 68-69
  early inhabitants, 50-51
  northern Andean region, 54-61
  Pampa, the, 66-67
  Patagonia, 68-69
  southern Andean region, 62-63
  Tierra del Fuego, 68-69
  Uruguay, 66-67
Southern Cult, 22
spear points, 6, 7, 16
step-pyramids, 57
Street of the Dead, 33, 34-35
subarctic regions, 4
subtropical plains, 4

## T

tablero, 33, 48
talud, 33, 48
Tehuelches, 66, 68
Temple of Agriculture, 33
Temple of Mythological Animals, 33
Temple of Quetzalcóatl, 33, 34-35
Temple of the Dancers, 42
Temple of the Warriors, 47
Temple of Tlahuizcalpantecuhtli, 36
Tenochtitlan, 37, 38-39
Teotihuacan, 33, 34-35
Tezcatlipocas, 37
theocratic, 14, 59
Thousand Columns, 47
Thule culture, 25
Tiahuanaco culture, 59
Tlaloc, 33, 37
tlaxtli, 48
Tobas, 66
Tollan, 36
Toltecs, 36-37, 47
tombac, 43
toolmaking, 5
tools, 7, 10, 16-17, 25, 27, 28, 32
Totonacs, 49
trade, 19, 65
tropical rain forests, 4
Tula, 36
tundra, 4, 26
Tupac Inca Yupanki, 60
Tupi-Guarani, 65
Tzolkin, 45

## V

Veracruz, 48-49
Veracruz Centre cultures, 48
Viking, 5
Viking Age, 5
villages, 10, 12-13, 17, 22, 30-31, 40-41

## W

weapons, 6, 16, 27, 28
weaving (see crafts)
woodworking, 10-11

## X

Xipe, 33
Xipe Totec, 37

## Z

Zapotecs, 42-43